"There are only a few books of the many thousands that I've read that change one's entire view of the world. Jeff Leiken has written one of those books. He starts with a simple assumption: there's nothing wrong with the adolescents he works with as a mentor. It's so simple that it's easy to miss the power of it, yet in his book he goes on to explain exactly why that's the only starting point that makes sense and then lays out the road map about what to do from there. If you're a parent or someone who works with teens, you need to read this book, and don't be surprised by how many times you feel that chill of recognition going up and down your spine."

—Joseph Riggio, PhD
International Executive Consultant
Architect and Designer, MythoSelf® Process
Author, *The State of Perfection*
Princeton, NJ

"In my years as CEO and Co-owner of *The Learning Annex*, I had the privilege of engaging with hundreds of prominent leading voices in the personal development field. I consider Jeffrey Leiken's work with adolescents and their parents, to be masterful.

Jeff Leiken's professional expertise, compassion, and understanding was a life-saving force that influenced our teen daughter to make better choices, and ultimately helped position and navigate her to a safer and more positive life path. I very highly endorse his work, especially if you have a teen who is more intense, more sensitive and seeking more out of life."

—Stephen Seligman
Former CEO and Co-owner of The Learning Annex

"It is rare to find someone who can dive right to the heart of the matter while making sure both the parent and teen feel heard and cared for. He has a highly effective, no BS approach (honest), supported by humor and a deep understanding of how teens and young adults work. He makes authentic connections, a mainstay of his program. I am so grateful to have someone with Jeff's skills as a resource. Each time I send him a family, I'm confident they are in good hands."

—Diane Provo, M.S. Ed.,
Parenting and Education Consultant
CEO, *Provo & Associates*
Coauthor, *Starting Blocks and Kids Are Great . . .*
When You Know How They Work
Larkspur, CA

"The greatest testimonial that I can offer for Jeff Leiken is that, after repeated years in which I hired him to work with our camp and youth organization, my wife and I ended up inviting him to be one of the primary mentors in our own teenage son's life. At a time when pundits and social critics speak of dark futures and diminishing options for our youth, Jeff offers a voice of practical optimism. Everything that Jeff stands for and teaches is based on the premise that each of our young people has the capacity to build a life that is true to themselves and their own core values. He does not offer untenable, abstract solutions but rather offers practical steps that are easy for any interested and motivated reader to understand and follow. As a professional in the youth development field for more than thirty years, a practitioner of this work myself, and most importantly and personally, as a father, I cannot endorse Jeff's work enough."

—Bobby Harris, M. Ed.
Director, URJ Camp Coleman and J-Jolt
(A URJ Mentoring and B'nai Mitzvah Initiative)
Atlanta, GA

"When I first started going to Jeff, it was not on my terms. My relationship with my parents when I was fifteen could be described as okay at best and, like many teenagers, intensely argumentative at worst, and they wanted me to 'see someone,' which would normally imply something clinical. But this was not the case. Working with Jeff has turned out to be the best gift my parents have given me throughout my teenage years and into my twenties. He is honest, observant, and does not beat around the bush with me. He helps me call out the habits that are keeping me stagnant and encourages a deeply thoughtful approach to living. If he doesn't know the answer or have the resources about a particular question, Jeff immediately reaches out to his extensive network of students, professionals, educators, and friends to get me the information that I need. He is my go-to person to call about complex life problems, romance confusion, and education or career decisions, and he has helped me see through the, for lack of a better word, bullshit of teenagers and adults in my world. Since meeting Jeff, I have become a much more 'real' person; at twenty-one, I am someone my fifteen-year-old self would look up to."

—Chloe Griffis

Bucknell University, Class of 2016

"Our son had run the gamut—Adderol, Zoloft, psychiatrists, tutors, drug counselors, treatment programs, you name it, he's done it. None of that has been effective in changing his attitudes or behaviors. Jeff doesn't cut him any slack, he doesn't make excuses for him, he just gives him straight talk - and holds him accountable. Our son is on the road to becoming a responsible adult and for that, I thank the one adult in his life he actually listens to—Jeff Leiken."

—Mark and Dee G.

Mill Valley, CA

"We had the good fortune of meeting Jeff Leiken when our daughter was thirteen. He was spending time at her summer camp where he was running a program for adolescents. We were impressed by his program and how effective he was helping these teens cope with the social pressures and challenges that teenagers regularly face, especially because it is so hard to find an adult who teens will actually listen to and take seriously. As a result, we decided to contact him privately.

Our daughter, who is now sixteen, and our family have benefited greatly from his ongoing support and advice. His patient and insightful approach to dealing with our daughter's complex adolescent issues, has been extremely effective. We have been overwhelmed by the way our daughter has opened up to Jeff and by his skillful way of maintaining her confidence while communicating openly and honestly with us as parents. We truly feel like we are a functional team with unified objectives and goals for our daughter. He has been an amazing resource and friend to our family."

—Pamela and Robert Friedman

Warren, NJ

"Jeff Leiken's work instills things that I have found are critical for young adults transitioning from college into career. Unfortunately as the Director of a Career Center, I meet too many students who lack these essential qualities and wind up struggling.

The method Jeff describes in this book helps adolescents develop a sense of who they are in the world. It builds the self-awareness and confidence that are critical components in ensuring success after school. By helping students find clarity and insight early on, it gives them an advantage in a complex world offering true value that reverberates long beyond adolescence."

—Jon Schlesinger, M.Ed., LPC

Director, Hiatt Career Center at Brandies University

Waltham, MA

"Jeffrey did for my daughter what I couldn't. Fitting in and seeking to be your own person at the same time is a difficult road to travel for a young twenty something. I quickly learned what Jeffrey told me was so true: He explained that my wife and I were advising our daughter quite well, however given what stage she was in her development, we were the wrong source. Jeffrey's exquisite mentoring plus his commitment to be available 24/7 achieved remarkable results. In just one year, she went from struggling with confidence, to boldly launching into her career and adult life."

—Michael Grottola
CEO, MGG CONSULTING
New York, New York

"Jeff Leiken is a passionate and dedicated teacher and coach for adolescents—an amazingly gifted practitioner and mentor. His work with middle and high school students has been magical to watch! As the cofounder of Beyond Differences, a nonprofit organization dedicated to ending social isolation among middle school students, I have been fortunate to partner with Jeff and see up close how he brings out the positive and personal power inside each student in our program to achieve their best. We are grateful to Jeff for his generosity in sharing his gifts with us."

—Laura Talmus
Executive Director and Cofounder, Beyond Differences
San Francisco, CA

"I originally came to Jeff as a highly athletic and driven fifteen-year-old with lofty career goals and a very lacking academic record. As Jeff and I met once a week, we were able to adjust my drive and motivation to help bolster my academics and rid my fear of not getting into a college. Now as a twenty-one-year-old student at the University of Arizona in the Naval Reserve Officer Training Corps, Jeff and I have run the gauntlet of ups, downs, and all arounds. We've covered dating, academics, mental blocks, career goals, part-time jobs, family issues, and just about anything else a teenager and young adult goes through. Every compass needs to be recalibrated, Jeff is the recalibration a compass needs."

—Austin Gooder
Novato, CA
University of Arizona 2017

"I had been searching for a few years for a program that could help my students at the college in developing lifelong skills in the areas of self-awareness, self-leadership, and self-actualization. When we found HeroPath, we had high hopes, but we could never have imagined how life changing it would become for many of our students. Our current student president, who arrived at the college as a shy sixteen-year-old and now, one year later, leads the entire student body attributes this achievement directly to attending the HeroPath program in his first year. I could cite countless other examples of students whose lives have been permanently enriched by attending the program and who have commended how the weekend was 'one of the greatest experiences of my life so far.'

I'm delighted to say that after the recent third successful program, we have decided to formally integrate HeroPath into the college curriculum for all students who want to attend. I am only sorry that more students elsewhere will not have the opportunity to experience it, but I am extremely proud that Oxford International College got there first in the UK!"

—Dr. Mario Peters
Director, Oxford International College
Oxford, England

"Jeff is not just outside the box when it comes to working with teens—he's redefining how we should think about it."

—Joshua Wayne
Creator, Your Successful Teen: The Complete Guide
to Turning Your Teen Into a Successful Young Adult
Washington, DC

"When I was in graduate school for clinical social work, fundamentally, everything we learned was about fixing people. Everyone who is clinically trained learns the same fundamental idea. Jeff never starts from a place of 'broken'; instead he starts from what works in our lives. From there, he is able to teach people to step onto the path that leads to their own personal excellence. The contrast between the conventional models and what he is doing couldn't be greater."

—Todd Kestin, LCSW
Mentor and Teen Life Coach
Huffington Post Contributor
Northbrook, IL

"Over the past twenty-three years, I have worked with over twenty thousand young people, and we have raised four children of our own. I have read a wide variety of parenting books and youth development theories. Jeff's approach to adolescence is a breath of fresh air. It is straightforward. It is optimistic. Most importantly, it gets remarkable results. Rather than see adolescence as a problem to be fixed, he recognizes opportunities to develop the skills and mind-sets needed to succeed. If you want an approach that will prepare your child for success, you need to read this book."

—Steve Baskin
Executive Director/Partner, Camp Champions,
Everwood Day Camp and Camp Pinnacle
Contributor, *Psychology Today*
Marble Falls, TX

"The first time I saw Jeff in action, I knew I had to bring him to Mexico to run a program for teens, parents, and professionals that work with teenagers. He surpassed all my expectations. The positive, humor-filled approach that Jeff brings to his work with teenagers is so refreshing! You can see the teens' resistance melt away and how they open up to new possibilities, new ideas, and a brighter future. I believe Jeff's work has a winning combination: a gift to work with teenagers and a methodology that truly works like nothing I have ever seen as a professional."

—Samantha Barachio
Psychologist and Certified Life Coach
Mexico City, MX

"Young people in today's society face issues that are difficult for parents to 'solve.' Our challenging world today is combined with the age-old difficulty that parents and teenagers experience in truly listening to one another. Jeff Leiken has a unique model that helps both parents and their teens. Jeff helped our son navigate through his teen years, and he is now on a path to become a thriving young adult. Jeff's availability to our son—by text and phone—made an enormous difference. Jeff supports and inspires young people as they grapple with the questions: 'Who am I? Who do I want to become? What are my dreams? What sort of mark do I want to leave on the world?'"

—Robert F. Epstein
San Rafael, CA

"When you have young children, they love you and believe everything you say is accurate. Then they become pre-teens and the questions begin about your authority. Then they become full fledge teenagers and questions of your authority, even your existence in their lives, develop! Where do you go from here?

Jeff Leiken came into our boys lives seven years ago, and his mentoring of our two sons has been invaluable. Our sons had very different personalities, ambitions and outlooks on life. Jeff was able to build a trusting relationship with each of them. He engaged them in the kind of dialogue that made them think about how they wanted to proceed in life.

When our highly competitive older son went through disappointing setbacks, Jeff helped train him to stay calm and focused. When our younger son struggled in a competitive Catholic High School, Jeff played an invaluable role helping him keep perspective and make excellent choices. When our marriage went through a turbulent time, Jeff went over and above to be there for us.

I cannot count the number of 7am or 11pm text messages he would respond to, or the urgent times he would make himself available.

Jeff is and will always be a part of our family even as my teenagers have grown into young men. I will always owe him a debt of gratitude for helping my boys and our family navigate the adolescent years. His genuine dedication to the families he works with is extraordinary. I cannot endorse him highly enough."

—Suzanne Barajas-Gooder

Novato, CA

"*In 2004, I attended a session Jeff led at a professional development conference. My wife and I had recently purchased a summer camp and were in the early years of finding our way.*

Whereas most other professional speakers offered feel-good formulaic 'one size fits all' solutions, Jeff spoke on a totally different level. The depth and sophistication of his message compelled me to speak with him afterwards. In that conversation, he boldly said one thing that made a powerful impact on my life. It was exactly what I needed to hear and has helped me to forge my own legacy, 'Making the world a better place— one client at a time.'

Jeff's work transcends the status-quo—the ordinary. If you are looking for ivy league statics, flashy degrees and 'media packaged experts' in the field, this is not the book for you. Instead, Jeff's book will help you guide your sons and daughters, on their journey, their path, removing the peripheral and unimportant, to point out what really matters. In the 12 plus years I have known Jeff—his platform has always been to look at 'what works' and to build from there. Jeff's book will help you or your teen to become the best version of yourself."

—Jim Gill
Owner/Director, Fernwood Cove Camp For Girls
Harrison, Maine

adolescence

IS ~~NOT~~ A

disease

adolescence

IS ~~NOT~~ A

disease

Beyond Drinking, Drugs,
and Dangerous Friends:
The Journey to Adulthood

Jeffrey Leiken, MA

Published by Advantage, Charleston, South Carolina.
Member of Advantage Media Group.

ADVANTAGE is a registered trademark and the Advantage colophon is a trademark of Advantage Media Group, Inc.

Printed in the United States of America.

ISBN: 978-1-59932-634-4
LCCN: 2015956807

This publication is designed to provide accurate and authoritative information in regard to the subject matter covered. It is sold with the understanding that the publisher is not engaged in rendering legal, accounting, or other professional services. If legal advice or other expert assistance is required, the services of a competent professional person should be sought.

 Advantage Media Group is proud to be a part of the Tree Neutral® program. Tree Neutral offsets the number of trees consumed in the production and printing of this book by taking proactive steps such as planting trees in direct proportion to the number of trees used to print books. To learn more about Tree Neutral, please visit www.treeneutral.com. To learn more about Advantage's commitment to being a responsible steward of the environment, please visit www.advantagefamily.com/green

Advantage Media Group is a publisher of business, self-improvement, and professional development books and online learning. We help entrepreneurs, business leaders, and professionals share their Stories, Passion, and Knowledge to help others Learn & Grow. Do you have a manuscript or book idea that you would like us to consider for publishing? Please visit advantagefamily.com or call 1.866.775.1696.

*Dedicated to my parents, Larry and Gail Leiken, and
to the memory of my grandparents, Harold and Minna
"Buddy" Brownstein and Ben and Millie Leiken.*

*And to all the wise elders who came before us, shared their
wisdom, gave back far more than they took, and on whose
shoulders we stand. May they rest in peace and their memory be
a blessing to all who knew them and whose lives they touched.*

"I Throw This Keylog in the
Fire to Thank..."

I spent sixteen summers of my youth at a boys summer camp in Northern Wisconsin. Each Friday night was campfire night. In addition to songs and stories, every campfire ended with a ritual "Keylog Ceremony." The idea of the Keylog came from a term used in the old days of the logging industry. When the logs were floated down the river, they would often jam up. It was the responsibility of one of the loggers to go out into the logjam and find the one log that all the others depended upon. Once that one was adjusted, all the rest were set free. That one log was called the keylog.

At our Keylog Ceremony, the boys would take a small piece of wood—a symbolic keylog—throw it in the fire, and offer their acknowledgments of those they depended upon, those who helped them, those who helped make their lives better.

In a typical book, this section is called the Acknowledgments. In this one, it will be my Keylog.

When I look over the history of my life, I can clearly see in retrospect several people who came into my life and quite literally opened up the world of my professional career. They are the people who are found at the beginning of the sequence of "If I hadn't met this person, I wouldn't have met that person, and if I hadn't met that person, I wouldn't have met ..." and so on.

The two people I want to gratefully acknowledge are Mike Cohen, owner and director of Camp Timberlane for Boys in Wisconsin, and

Larry Palmatier, my professor from graduate school at the University of San Francisco School of Education.

Both eventually became my teacher, my boss, my client, my colleague, and my friend.

When Mike bought the camp in 1985, he revamped the orientation training, bringing a professionalism and seriousness to the "counselor" part of the job "camp counselor." When Mike taught skills and theory, I was captivated with learning for the first time in my life and only wanted to learn more. That summer, I discovered my fascination. Over the years, Mike gave me the chance to become a professional. He challenged me to work harder than I'd ever worked before and gave me my first chance to be a leader. He also gave me my first chance to teach others. The opportunity he gave me to help train his staff, and his introduction to Bob Ditter, opened the door to my now having worked with over three hundred summer camps and presented to over thirty thousand professionals in the youth development industry, especially in the American Camp Association. Nearly every contact to speak at a conference or work with an organization can be linked back to the opportunity and introductions Mike made for me.

I met Larry Palmatier when I was still an undergraduate student. I used to sneak myself into graduate classes because I was eager to learn. Larry was the head of the Educational Counseling Department and a veteran professor in the Counseling Psychology Department at USF. Larry was one of the most brilliant, honorable, congruent teachers and men I'd ever met. He was among the best in the world at what he did with the work of William Glasser and The Quality School model. It was his vision of educational counseling that persuaded the faculty to allow a course in neuro-linguistic programming to be taught in a masters program. At the time, his was the only graduate program in the world to offer this. The connection I made with the teacher of that course led to me meeting Colleen Newlin, who shortly thereafter introduced me to Joseph Riggio, the teacher and mentor who changed my life, inspired HeroPath, and connected me with the world—quite literally, every international program I've ever run can be linked to something Joseph taught me or someone I met through him. Because of Joseph, I met Des Barry, my colleague and friend who helped build HeroPath from a simple idea concocted over a latte in a London cafe, to an internationally acclaimed program which we've now run on three continents, with more in the works. Thank you to Joseph and Des.

Larry also later hired me to teach graduate school at the University of San Francisco. It was in that capacity that I met Laura Weiss, who later invited me to run mentoring groups at Mill Valley Middle School. That introduction and contact led to the practice and most of the vast range of connections I now have, both in Northern California and beyond.

Larry left us way too soon. My memories of him and the impact he had on my life stay with me years later and will forever. I truly do not know who I would be, where I would be, or what I would be doing had I not met Larry. Thank you, Larry. Thank you, thank you, thank you.

Mike and I continue to stay connected thirty years later, maintaining a relationship of deep mutual professional respect and an abiding friendship that sustains, even though he is a lifelong St. Louis Cardinals fan and I was born and bred a die-hard Cubs fan. Just goes to show you that anything is possible... yes Mike, even a Cubs World Series.

Because of these two men, the list of people to thank is so much longer. What a gift to have people in my life to be thankful for. So thanks to the following incredible innovators, thought-leaders, camp leaders, educators, and parents who have contributed in a very direct and substantial way to the realizations and experience this book draws upon: Thank you to Ric and Lisa Capretta, Rob and Lisa Epstein, Michael Grottolla, Whitney Hoyt, Anna Lazzarini, David and Allison Miller, Adam Baker, Bobby Harris, Scott Brody, Jason Sebell, Bruce Lipton, Jim and Beigette Gill, Steve and Susie Baskin, Tiffany Romero, Michael Cage, Dennis Charles, Mark Schwimmer, Todd Kestin, Cousin Brian Leiken, Helen Morris Ferguson, and my brother, Joshua Wayne.

Lastly, as we live our lives, we just never know what role different people will play or how we will meet.

In my early thirties, I was dating voraciously, doing a lot of making up for lost time, and searching for a pathway out of the loneliness of bachelorhood, in spite of my own fears of commitment.

I met Robyn Kohn through J-Date, an Internet dating site, in July of 2002. She showed up for our first date nearly two hours late. With no cell phone or GPS, she'd missed a turn and wound up driving all the way to the ocean. When she finally showed up, I walked around the corner, laid eyes on this redhead, and a chill went up my spine, accompanied by these words in my head: "There's something different about this one."

Try as hard as I might to screw things up, our life paths eventually brought us back together again in the fall of 2003, over a year later. The day I answered that next call from her, I knew that I would marry her. I'm glad I answered The Call.

We now have two daughters, Peyton and Skylar. Like their mom, they are beautiful, sensitive, charismatic, and soulful.

My wife tolerates a lot to be married to me. She accommodates my crazy work schedule; all my travel; my clients who call, Skype, text, and show up at my doorstep 24/7 every day of the year; and the ups and downs of being married to an entrepreneur.

Robyn, you are a far greater woman, wife, and mother than your humility and self-standards allow you to realize. I am humbled by your patience, your nurturance, and your conviction to live true to your principles. Both our daughters and I are lucky to have you in our lives.

I thank Robyn, Peyton, and Skylar, not just for their patience with me through the process of writing this book but for reminding me that nothing matters to the world the way that being a husband and father matters to my family or that being a spouse and parent matters in every family.

I hope I can get it right.

TABLE OF CONTENTS

PART 1

AN UPDATED, TIMELY PERSEPCTIVE ON ADOLESCENCE, PARENTING, and HELPING YOUTH ON THEIR JOURNEY TO ADULTHOOD:

How to Become the Expert on Being a Parent

PART 2

THE THREE STAGES OF ADOLESCENCE WHAT'S GOING ON, WHY & HOW TO TRULY HELP

Introduction

As soon as my children were old enough to speak, they knew the answers to two questions:

#1: "What is Mom and Dad's number one job?"

Answer: "To keep me safe."

#2: What is Mom and Dad's number two job?"

Answer: "To help me thrive."

The line "Remember what my number one job is!" has been used many times when our kids were disappointed that I didn't say yes to something that seemed safe enough to them. But more importantly, these words were a mantra for me to remind myself of what my role as a parent must be: to prepare our children to thrive in a complex, chaotic, and rapidly changing world in spite of systems that are often ill designed to meet their deeper needs.

When our children are young, we as parents are the centers of their world. Raising them in early childhood is a constellation of joyous moments, interspersed with agonizing frustration, often depending on how hungry or tired they are … or on how hungry or tired we are. But the joy typically far outweighs the agony. Then school age arrives, and suddenly the outside world becomes a much bigger influence in their lives. Most parents can recall the first time their child came home from school, saying something they'd heard in the world out there or telling a story about a child who did something cruel to them. All too many parents can also remember the first time they got a call from school because their child did something they never thought their child would do.

This marks the beginning of a different phase of parenthood. The cacophony of opinions and biases of media, peers, and other adults begins to build up inside our kids, often giving them messages and tempting or influencing them to do things that we disagree with and don't want for them. At that point, we must work harder and be more proactive to keep our children on track—yet often it is at this point that parents begin struggling to keep up. This book is for every parent who has faced this struggle and who is ready for a fresh perspective, one that instills hope, re-empowers parents, and helps them break free from the fear-based system and messages that dominate the current discourse on parenting.

I see a lot of irrationality and fear clouding the thinking and decision making of modern parents. That's not surprising, given that we've become a culture that devours best-selling books that, buttressed with research, give us all sorts of conflicting advice about how to raise our kids properly. What's the right way to handle our toddler's tantrums, food issues, learning challenges, and so on? Do we vaccinate? Do we breastfeed? Do we let them cry it out, or do we pick them up and soothe them? Do we force them to stay on the team to teach them a lesson about commitment, or do we respect that they've lost interest and let them quit? Do we tell our teens about our own experiences with drugs and sex, or do we not? Do we let them struggle with friend problems, or do we step in and handle them for them? Do we teach them to read when they are five, or do we wait until they are naturally curious and risk letting them fall behind their peers?

Other expert-endorsed books tell us what common sense already should have: that spoiling kids is bad, that children need to exercise and play outdoors, and that our sons and daughters can still have amazing careers even if they don't get into Harvard. Are we at the point where we need experts to tell us what we all already know, either instinctively or through our own life experience? Sadly, the answer would appear to be yes—because so many parents, out of fear or ignorance, have stopped trusting themselves or have given too much of the responsibility of raising their kids over to institutions.

It's not that all institutions are bad or wrong. It is that each child is unique, and no one institution or approach is right for everyone.

Perhaps the wisest person I ever met on the topic of parenting was a stranger I sat next to on a flight from San Francisco to Atlanta a few years ago. This elderly woman noticed the book I was editing—a book I'd written on a program for boys becoming young men. She shared with me how she too had written a book on raising boys, a book her niece had inspired her to write. Her story was that her husband had died tragically when her three sons were young, leaving her penniless. In spite of these challenges, she still raised her three boys to become highly educated and accomplished men. She was on her way back home, having just visited one of her sons, a surgeon at Stanford University Medical Center.

> Many parents, out of fear or ignorance, have stopped trusting themselves or have given too much of the responsibility of raising their kids over to institutions.

"People often hear my story and tell me, 'You must be an expert on raising boys.' 'No,' I tell them, 'I'm not an expert on raising boys. Just my own!'"

I love that story.

I believe in her wisdom. I hope through this book to help every parent step outside the limitations of the conventional thinking of the educational, psychological, medical, and political systems that dominate our current culture, empowering them to become experts in raising their own children, specifically through their teen years transitioning into young adulthood ... to help them find the ways to draw out the best in their sons and daughters, equipping them to thrive even in the chaotic and rapidly changing world they are inheriting.

Teen rebellion, dangerous risk taking, and impulsive decision making are not the unavoidable "normal" developmental behaviors they have been made out to be, nor are they evidence of mental illness or character disorders. They are common behaviors we too often see in adolescents, typically as a by-product of having to come of age in the current system, as are the other, more concerning behaviors that parents worry about, like bouts of intense anxiety or drug use progressing from social experimentation to self-medication.

Waiting until bad things happen before we honestly address the inner lives of our adolescents is a very poor strategy and a very costly one. The longer parents put off becoming proactive, the more likely it is that those kinds of things not only will happen but will become problems.

It doesn't have to be this way.

Being proactive requires recognizing that adolescents have particular needs that must be met, different from what they had as children or that we have as adults. In this book I lay out a model of what goes on in the journey from being a child to becoming an adult. This journey has three distinct stages—each with its own driving concerns and underlying developmental questions that need answers—and a virtual question that needs resolution. This book explores each stage in depth because what is needed and how to help varies according to the stage.

Stage 1 begins around puberty, typically twelve years old or seventh grade in the US education system. It is the stage of awakening to the social world—the quest to be cool and fit in, the physical changes and raging hormones, and the awkwardness of adjusting to the newfound social world. "Mom, leave me alone ... I can do it myself ... *I'm not a kid any more!*" is their collective cry. The driving question at this stage is "Am I cool enough to be socially accepted and desired?" Stage 1 is fixated on "Where do I fit in in the world of my peers?"

Stage 2 begins between fifteen and a half and seventeen years old, when teens typically go through a major awakening. Up until then, they have only been who they have been told to be, or who they had to be to gain approval and acceptance of parents and peers, but at this stage they suddenly realize that they are their own person. The driving question now becomes "Who am I really?" Stage 2 is ultimately about *"Where do I fit in in the bigger world?"*

Stage 3 begins in the late teen years to early twenties. It is the stage of stepping into the adult world, starting a career, and/or moving into independent adult life. It is the leap into 100 percent commitment. The driving question is "Am I ready?" Often, it's "Am I good enough?"

Using real-life examples from teens and young adults with whom I've had the privilege to work over the last three decades, I detail the ways these stages of adolescence are experienced inside of youth, as well as what works to help them through these stages and to evolve into responsible, capable, thriving adults. The teens and young adults whose stories I relate in this book range in age from twelve to twenty-six and come from places as far-reaching as New Zealand and the Middle East, with the majority coming from the United States and Europe, where I do the bulk of my work.

They draw on the model of work I call Evolution Mentoring, a methodology I cultivated and developed through over fifty thousand hours of experience, much of which involved unraveling the conventional counseling and psychological training I received early in my career. Rather than subscribe to the dominant paradigm that pathologizes, diagnoses, and treats struggling adolescents as if there were something wrong with them, I take a very different approach based on a very different premise: I presume there is nothing wrong with them. In most cases, what is really going on is that life suddenly grows more complex and confusing when puberty and the teen years begin, and many youth are simply not equipped to understand and manage it, leading to stress and stress reactions.

To make matters worse, many parents either are so consumed with managing their own complex lives or become so focused on their teen's grades and building a college or job application resume that they fail to find the time to really help them, or worse, fail to see or appreciate the significance of the inner journey that their son or daughter is now on—a journey that could be magical and exciting but instead becomes stressful and angst-ridden.

For all the advances we have made in understanding human life, adolescence is one area where we seem to have taken huge leaps backward. Nowhere is this more glaringly obvious than in the volume of teens whose lives are so disrupted by stress-related issues that they are receiving medication, psychological treatment, and clinical mental health care just to help them make it through the adolescent years.

The numbers are disturbing: one in eight boys are now on ADD medication; one in eleven adolescents are receiving clinical mental heath treatment (in some cases this is warranted, but in many others it's an overreaction); nearly 60 percent of college freshman will not graduate in six years, and nearly 30 percent will not even return for their sophomore year, mostly because they were ill equipped to manage the responsibilities and freedoms of being away from home. The rate of adolescents diagnosed with mental health disorders has doubled in the last decade, as have the numbers of those taking prescription drugs.

> For all the advances we have made in understanding human life, adolescence is one area where we seem to have taken huge leaps backward.

Cultures throughout time understood this stage of life far better than ours does. They appreciated the value of offering teens emerging and awakening into adulthood—intellectually, sexually, physically, and spiritually—the proper opportunities, challenges, experiences, relationships, and lessons that would enable them to complete the transformation from being a child to becoming an adult.

In today's world, though, instead of receiving this comprehensive, in-depth immersion and growth into adulthood, most adolescents have been forced for the last century to sit in classrooms, learning things they will mostly never use, deprived of creativity, disconnected from adults, and worrying about how their ability or inability to measure up academically will equate to the brightness or bleakness of their future, while simultaneously having the same worries about their social future. Meanwhile, their minds wander, their souls seek, and their bodies yearn for challenge and connection. Yet they could so easily be reached if only the adults around them knew how—and before they give up and give in.

Knowing how to do this begins with the adults in their lives asking the right questions and understanding and appreciating a few often overlooked considerations—some that are timeless and a few that are timely—which can make an enormous difference in how well these questions get answered.

Here are a few of the popularly held beliefs and practices that often keep youth from evolving into thriving young adults:

1) *We need to help adolescents keep their options open.* Wrong. We want to help them begin eliminating choices that are not right for them, the sooner the better. This will significantly increase the quality of their decision making.

2) *We need to help adolescents get into the best colleges.* Wrong. We need to help them get into the right programs for them, which may or may not be at the top of the list of elite schools and may even mean not going to college at all.

3) *We need to help adolescents find their passion and their purpose.* Wrong. Few people ever find the "one thing" they feel they were put on this earth to do, often not even having a remote experience of this until they become a parent. Rarely do those who do find something they love enough that they would suffer for it (which I consider to be a more evolved definition of passion than the

feel-good one that has been embraced in the popular self-help movement) find that it is something they can readily make a living doing. It is far more valuable to help adolescents identify their strengths and interests and to build a life that flows from these. (We built our HeroPath program specifically to help older teens and young adults do this: www.HeroPath.life.)

4) *Drinking, drugs, and sex are stepping-stones to maturity.* Wrong. Too often the questions of drugs, drinking, and sex are treated as a matter of "when," not "if." Maturity comes from treating all these things as a matter of "if," not "when," and then doing these things only if and when adolescents feel it is the right time for them. There is no universal life checklist for what people need to do and when they need to do it.

5) *We need to make sure they have a backup plan.* Jimi Hendrix didn't have one. Michael Jordon didn't. For someone who is going to pursue a line in which it's difficult to achieve financial success, they must give it their all and must persist even when it gets tough—even if they have to do it while waiting tables in the off hours.

There is no "one size fits all" program that works for everyone. Parents need to work to bring together the right team and the opportunities to help each of their children. But the one thing that is universally true is that adolescence is not a disease.

PART ONE

AN UPDATED, TIMELY PERSEPCTIVE
ON ADOLESCENCE, PARENTING,
AND HELPING YOUTH ON THEIR
JOURNEY TO ADULTHOOD:

*How to Become the
Expert on Being a Parent*

chapter
one

The Single Most Important Question Every Parent Needs to Find the Right Answers To

What must my children learn, know, and be able to
do to ensure they'll grow up to thrive in today's world?
And how and when will they learn these things?

There are three categories of answers to this question, and all three must be successfully addressed to ensure that each child thrives now and as they evolve into adulthood.

1) What learning and capabilities are timeless and universally needed? (e.g., basic literacy, social skills, etc.)

2) What learning and capabilities are timely, given the realities of today's world? (e.g., the ability to use and wisely navigate the realm of technology, the ability to engage multiculturally, etc.)

3) What learning and capabilities are going to be needed that are unique and idiosyncratic to each individual child based on who they are and their temperament, interests, strengths, weaknesses, needs, ambitions, and circumstances?

As simple as the questions may be to answer, they are often far more difficult to effectively act on and address. Our educational system is so limited in scope, and often so one dimensional, that alone it plays only a limited role in helping prepare youth for real-life success. It takes far more than school.

In recent decades, breakthroughs in understanding the development of the human brain point to a lack of consistent access to the frontal lobes as the reason a teen might do something brilliant one moment and then ten minutes later make the stupidest, most impulsive decision imaginable. Books based on this research suggest that brain wiring is to blame for teens' high-risk behaviors and poor time management despite those moments of brilliance. What both the research and those books fail to take into account is a critical variable: context. What would happen if the brains of the rare teens who have been given ample opportunity to face real challenges, handle responsibilities, have deep, connected relationships, and contribute substantively in their world were compared to the well-researched brains of typical Western teens who have spent seven hours a day for twelve years in conventional classrooms with little physical movement and few meaningful, substantive challenges, coupled with massive academic and social stress, all while being frequently bored, repressed, and coerced into compliance and submission?

I'm neither a brain researcher nor a neuroscientist, so I can't tell you how their brains would differ if we looked inside. But I can tell you a lot about how the rare teens described above would look and behave on the outside. I have seen countless examples of what happens when adolescents are given the developmentally appropriate training, opportunities, guidance, and input that they really need, at the time and in the ways they most need it. Evolution Mentoring (www.EvolutionMentoring.com), the model this book is based on, has produced substantial positive results with both some of the most at-risk youth from our worst inner cities and some of the most stressed-out youth from our nation's most competitive and affluent communities and has benefited just about every kind of teen and young adult in between. It has guided them to assume greater responsibility for their lives, to be more discerning in their relationships, to consistently take on healthy challenges, and to make smarter decisions, thereby both ensuring their maturation and ensuring that they will develop potency to make an impact in their world—exactly what this stage of life should be doing for them.

This approach works so well for two big reasons: (1) it is positively biased (meaning it builds on their strengths and focuses on possibilities) and (2) it proactively addresses the real inner needs that teens and young adults have, both the needs that are universal and those that are idiosyncratic to each individual—almost all of which must be met and addressed outside the domain of academic classrooms.

"When I Was Your Age…"

Yes, we were all once their age. We all know the growing pains and shifting hormones of puberty—from acne to mood swings to joint pains, harder homework and competition, and either watching our friends get taller or grow breasts sooner or developing before them and having to awkwardly adjust to a new body and being seen as different. Then there are the first pangs of sexual desire, the first crushes and yearnings to connect romantically, the first time you looked in the mirror and questioned if you were "cool enough" after a childhood in which this notion never entered your mind… The list of universal experiences is extensive.

In addition to experiences like these that are the same for all teens, there are also experiences that are different for each individual—and to really understand the inner world of your teen today, the differences matter.

What's in the News Matters

For many of today's youth—the millennial generation as we commonly call it, and more recently "Generation Z" (children born since the early 2000s who've been raised knowing how to use an iPhone before they know how to read)—their inherent sense of magic, adventure, and discovery has been sadly diminished. Rather than seeing their future as something exciting to be explored, they see it as something to be worried about. Instead of a quest to thrive, for many now the goal is simply to survive. It used to be enough to be in the top third of their class, but now many feel they must be in the top 1 percent. And rather than this transition happening when they are ready to contribute—typically by sixteen years old—the demands of schooling consumes their time and delays their deep desire and need to contribute, challenge themselves, accomplish, and deeply connect.

As of the writing of this book, it has been nearly fifteen years since 9/11, eleven years since *An Inconvenient Truth* was released (Al Gore's monumental documentary about the damage of global warming), seven years since "the worst economic collapse since the Great Depression," and six years since the phrase "one percenters" was coined. The recent terrorist attacks in Egypt and Paris only add to the list of reasons to feel unsafe and uncertain about the world. Today's youth have come of age in a decade dominated by bad news.

Contrast this with the decade in which Gen Xers like myself came of age. The 1980s began with a simple event that came to symbolize a decade of massive revolution: In February 1980, barely seven weeks into the decade, a group of young college hockey players joined together, went to a small town in upstate New York, and pulled off the single greatest upset in the history of modern sports. "Do you believe in miracles?" became the rallying cry for the decade. Team USA's defeat of the USSR's hockey team, which had previously dominated the sport worldwide, occurred at the dawn of a decade that began steeped in the Cold War and the fear and threat of nuclear war and ended with the collapse of the Berlin Wall in 1989, sealing the fate and collapse of the "evil" Soviet empire. That began a nearly twenty-year period dominated by the spread of freedom and democracy (Nelson Mandela's election as president of South Africa in 1994 was probably the most profound evidence of hope), economic expansion (the Clinton legacy of character flaws is endlessly overlooked because of the years of economic growth during his presidency), the technological revolution (where information and opportunity that had been reserved for an elite few became accessible to all, and what seemed like a consistent positive movement in social and scientific evolution. My generation graduated college with little to no debt, quickly got jobs, and got on with our adult lives.

That sense of limitless possibility came crashing to earth one Tuesday morning in September of 2001.

What has happened since has been an almost constant stream of events and news pointing in the opposite direction. Instead of the mind-set being "anything is possible" and "the journey is the destination," many young people believe that there is increasing scarcity due to declining resources and opportunity. This is reflected overwhelmingly in the wildly popular dystopian books and movies that have raked in billions of millennial dollars in the last decade. From *Harry Potter*, to *The Hunger Games*, to *Maze Runner*, to popular sci-fi films that depict a future where only the uber-wealthy have life's comforts and the masses are left to forage in bleak scarcity. These stories continually depict a dichotomy between the untrustworthy adults (mostly politicians, big business people, and scientists), who in their greed have caused the problems, versus the young teen hero who will lead the revolt against them. Sure, they inspire a generation of mythological teen heroes, much as Luke Skywalker did forty years ago. An important difference, though, is that Katniss (the hero of *The Hunger Games*) is fighting an evil enemy who lives right down the street, whereas Luke Skywalker fought an evil empire in a distant galaxy. One is a lot more "real" and relatable than the other.

Too many of today's youth come of age with a sense that nearly everything is a competition, whether simply to survive in a world that doesn't make it easy for them, as inner-city youth like those I worked with in the 1990s still experience, or in competition to get to the top 1 percent, as many of the youth I write about in this book experience, who've been led to believe that is their only hope of security and, yes, personal happiness. One high-achieving high school junior told me that "my school is a cesspool of diseases because everyone is too afraid to miss classes and risk falling behind, so they come to school sick and get everyone else sick, and we all just keep passing it around."

This sense of fear and scarcity often extends to parents and even stems from them, leading them to be as immersed in their kids' schooling as the kids are themselves. Actual learning or preparation for managing real life often takes a distant back seat to building the resume required for entrance to top-tier colleges—those perceived as connected enough to give graduates a chance to be more than middle-of-the-road, disposable workers. Real-life experience overwhelmingly shows us that success in any career and business can and does happen regardless of where we go to college (or even *if* we go to college in many cases), yet the current mythology of elitism seems to ignore this, placing inordinate amounts of stress and pressure on the illusion that where they go to college matters far more than it actually does. Colleges themselves struggle with the reality that 30 percent of incoming freshmen nationwide leave school after one year, as they are often either ill prepared or too burned out after high school to stay focused and manage the responsibilities.

A high school senior called me last Saturday because he was distraught that he didn't get into Duke University. The fact that he got into nine other highly regarded schools was not a consolation, because of how much meaning he'd placed on what it meant to his life to go to that one. By the time we were done talking, he'd chilled out, reconnected with gratitude to be in a position to even go to college without having to take out loans and was once again excited about the adventure that lay ahead for him, not at Duke but instead at Northwestern. Other than their basketball programs and colder winter, this was certainly not a step down. For his major, it was actually arguably a step up. His story of feeling distraught over not getting into a top-choice school and feeling he was "settling instead" for a different, still prestigious school, is not uncommon among this demographic of the teen population. It is also absurd to worry that much about something like this.

Bucket Lists

While causing them added stress about their futures, this sense of scarcity has also led many millennials to prioritize having what were previously cherished as "once-in-a-lifetime" type experiences now, instead of the time-held tradition of waiting to have them later in life. Instead of collecting wealth, these youth aim to collect experiences.

One of the most popular books and gurus of the early millennials (the ones now in their late-twenties to mid-thirties) was *The 4-Hour Work Week*, in which Tim Ferriss explained how to leverage inexpensive labor from third world countries to do their work for them, to create what have become known as "bucket lists" (experiences they want to have before they "kick the bucket"), and to save enough money to go do what they want now instead of waiting for retirement. In the introduction to the book, Ferriss tells how he found a loophole in the rules of a Chinese kickboxing tournament that allowed him to win matches by shoving competitors out of the ring. He claims to have used this to win a national championship in the sport even though he didn't know how to

> Instead of collecting wealth, these youth aim to collect experiences.

kickbox. He was one of the founding voices of the popular interest among millennials in finding "life hacks," or shortcuts, to get results.

While Ferriss may have won a national title by finding this "hack" in the rules and exploiting it, my immediate reaction in reading it was to wonder what would happen were he to be confronted by one of those opponents in a back alleyway where the tournament rules didn't apply but the ability to actually kickbox did. I imagine him in a bloody heap, doubled over, clutching his trophy as he hung on for dear life.

Getting results without putting in the effort to earn it through hard work and honest effort is a value that is in stark contrast to the value that most in my generation were raised with: the value of earning your rewards the old-fashioned way, by putting in the hours and effort to actually become good at something—the timeless pathway to mastery. Parents need to understand that finding shortcuts is not only encouraged by today's youth peer culture, it is overwhelmingly valued by it. This commonly shows up in things like taking other people's prescription ADD meds to help them do better on exams, cheating in school (nearly 75 percent of high school and college students admit to cheating, including at elite schools, where famous studies were done on this), taking steroids to help them improve athletic performance, or pirating entertainment media from various sites on the internet where they can illegally gain access without having to pay. The attitude seems to be: *It's not what you had to do to get where you wanted to get to, what matters is that you got there.*

This kind of attitude—doing questionable things without guilt— makes perfect sense for people who see life as a competition for limited resources and opportunities—people who feel they are just doing what they have to do to stay alive. It borders on offensive, though, for any of us who were raised with a sense of traditional morality, of right and wrong, and with an appreciation of the innate rewards of hard work and a job well done, and the moral code of agreeing to play fairly. To really understand and relate to today's youth, it is critical to realize that every time the message is repeated to them about how scarce the opportunities are and how critical it is to get elite grades to get a 1 percenter job, we are only reinforcing the justification that many youth use for these behaviors.

> Parents need to understand that finding shortcuts is not only encouraged by today's youth peer culture, it is overwhelmingly valued by it.

The Interpersonal Toll

The impact of this goes much deeper for them personally, though, because of an unavoidable by-product of living this way: it creates mistrust among them. And yet, trust is essential to making deep connections. Many share their stories with me of how it is common to learn that their friends have lied to them and prove to be unreliable. I commonly hear stories of how they found out their friends lied to them saying they had to stay home and have dinner with family, when in fact they blew them off to go out with other friends to a better party. "The worst is when they lie to me and then I see the whole truth being played out on Instagram and Snapchat!" one seventeen-year-old told me as she was deciding what to do after discovering the lies that had been told to her.

The current attitude that endorses sexual promiscuity, "hooking up" as it is commonly called, comes at a cost as well. "The fraternity guys at my school have it made," one college student told me recently. Because the school she goes to in Pennsylvania doesn't allow the girls to live together in sorority houses but does allow boys to have fraternity houses, "Basically every weekend, the guys just host a party and sit back and wait for a bunch of drunk sorority girls to come over and at the end of the night sleep with them. There is no shame in staying the night there and doing it with one guy one night and another the next… It's just the stuff we all sit around and talk and text about the next day and the things you do to keep getting invited to more parties." What she later revealed to me—and what will become evident further into this book—is how unsettling, unsatisfying, and destabilizing this lifestyle is. As she also confided, "Every time I do this, I wake up the next morning and just feel so used."

Sexual Dysfunction in Teens

I cannot count the number of times the adolescents I work with have confided in me the fears they have about their sexuality. I hear from healthy young men who either can't get erections when they are with girls or can't ejaculate while having sex or from girls who are wondering if they are lesbians or are asexual because they find no pleasure in the sexual experiences they are having with boys. I have to explain to them the merits of actually trusting the person they are with so they can be fully relaxed and how what they see in porn is not a reflection of what sexual intimacy is really like. The degree of detail the conversations must go into would probably make some people uncomfortable, but the relief it provides

> "Every time I do this, I wake up the next morning and just feel so used."

them to know they can trust themselves and know they are okay—and that it is okay to wait either for the right person or the right time in life—has solved a lot of "sexual dysfunction" issues. I'm often teaching them that they will be far more satisfied (and functional) when they let the degree of sexual contact they have with a partner only match the degree of trust, comfort, and intimacy they feel with that person in every nonphysical way, too. It's proven a remarkable formula for helping them launch into healthy, thriving intimate relationships.

At the risk of overgeneralizing, let me be clear: Sure, there have always been "players" and "cheaters," even thirty years ago. Many successful adults today rationalize unethical behavior in the workplace with the argument that "business is business." The difference, though, is that generally speaking, most of us who grew up at that time shared a common moral compass that pointed toward a universal constant, regardless of what religion or background we came from: treat others the way you want to be treated. Not everyone lived up to that, and we all have moments we miss the mark. But today's youth often lack this focus point because it requires believing enough in the future, trusting in something greater than themselves, and trusting that others will do the same. Instead they frequently feel that if they aren't doing what it takes to compete, even if competing requires moral compromise, the only thing that will happen is that they will lose.

There is a time and place to update some of the "traditional values" our generation was raised with. Recent research on the merits of THC (the active agent in marijuana) certainly does present a bold case for its potential to be legitimately medicinal and for the idea that the policy of treating it like a dangerous drug is overblown. And almost universal access to spell-check, auto-calculations, and access to information creates a strong argument as to why learning how to do complex calculations in our heads or to spell rarely used words correctly by sight no longer needs to be emphasized in education. The list grows.

> There is a time and place to update some of the "traditional values" our generation was raised with.

But some things are universal: Trust is essential in building healthy relationships. Hard and persistent work is essential to achieving excellence in anything and, as an added pressure now, is required in order to remain relevant in a rapidly changing world. And collecting self-fulfilling experiences on a bucket list is, in the end, no more deeply satisfying than having made a lot of money. In other words, both may feel good, but neither has much to do with achieving deep human contentment and happiness, which still come as a well-earned by-product of making commitments, connections, and contributions.

The Good News

There are still many modern youth who do subscribe to more traditional values about relationships, work ethic, and the path to success. Parents who are raising one of these youth should be sensitive to how disconcerting it can be for them to have to contend with classmates who cheat or how they might feel as if they are in the minority because they don't do drugs or have frivolous sex. They need reinforcement that staying true to themselves is *always* worth it, even if it takes them a little more effort to find the right people and their path to success.

Even those who have gotten jaded by the scarcity and competition mentality are often remarkably reachable. Their cynicism about the world, particularly about relationships with peers, is often just a coping mechanism: if they lower their expectations enough, then they can't be disappointed. Not far beneath that front, they can often easily regain the sense of hope, creativity, and possibility they were born with ... it is their birthright, as it is all of ours. Accessing it is easy: just watch any of a million inspirational TED Talks or YouTube videos and anyone will experience a moment of hope. The far greater and more important task—and what has become the focus of my own life work—has been to teach them to live this way as a way of life, not as a result of a motivational talk. This way, rather than it being a temporary high, it becomes a high-quality approach to life.

The challenge for forward-thinking parents, then, becomes how to keep their kids feeling positive, centered, focused, prepared to succeed, and morally driven, even when others around them seem not to be. How do we help them succeed at the game without selling their souls for it? How do we ensure their deeper developmental needs are addressed and met, while managing the rest of the craziness that masquerades as education for real-life success? One of the universal constants in answering these questions is realizing that this is not done alone—that it takes a village—and that presuming that all will somehow work out fine for them because it did for you is not a wise presumption to make.

Have faith, be positive, yet don't get caught up in expecting your teens to readily buy into the old-school traditional values you committed to in the past. Simultaneously, don't be blinded by what looks like success. No matter how well they may be doing in school, there is a whole inner journey going on, rife with trials and challenges that cannot be measured by standardized tests, yet that matter as much now as ever. Often, the best support we can give is aiding that journey because developing savvy, sophistication, maturity, and character on the inside will enable them to thrive in spite of what happens on the outside. Fortunately, their innate sense of curiosity and adventure, just like our own, continues to remain intact and quickly re-emerges when encouraged, nourished, and reinforced. Doing this demands continuing to see and believe in the best in them, even when

The challenge for forward-thinking parents, then, becomes how to keep their kids feeling positive, centered, focused, prepared to succeed, and morally driven, even when others around them seem not to be.

they do things that are anything but their best, as all humans are prone to do. This is how to best ensure that those moments or phases in life do not define who they become but rather just play a small role in their realization of becoming the best of who they have the potential to be.

chapter
two

Beyond Punishment and Lectures:
"Should I Be Concerned?"

Fifteen-year-old Carly left her phone on the kitchen counter after dinner. Her mom innocently picked it up, intending to bring it to Carly, when she glanced down and, to her dismay, saw things on it that were anything but innocent. Carly's "private" Instagram account was open, and the images it revealed shocked her mom: graphic pictures of Carly drinking, smoking weed, and passed out. They'd been taken at her friend's birthday party Saturday night, the same party that she had told her mom was "just a few girls having dinner and a sleepover." As her mom scrolled further, she read text messages about hooking up with boys and a confession to a friend about how "I can't believe I did that..." The messages went back all the way to the beginning of the summer, almost five months before. What should her parents have done when they discovered that Carly was not only not innocent but potentially putting herself at great risk?

Seventeen-year-old Daniel got into his first-choice college early admission. He had a great girlfriend and a solid family, was the captain of his soccer team, and would be playing soccer in college. He had everything going for him—so why was he having panic attacks and such severe anxiety that he couldn't sleep at night? How should his parents have reacted? How concerned should they have been?

Thirteen-year-old Brooke went to school the first day of eighth grade and heard all about the sleepovers that happened over the summer with her best friends from seventh grade—all of which happened without her being invited or ever knowing about them. The seat at the lunch table that had always been reserved for her was suddenly no longer available. Two weeks into the school year, she broke down in tears with her parents, telling them about what was going on. She cried nonstop for several hours. Her parents had never seen her this upset. Should they call the other girls' parents? Should they tell the school about it? Should they get her professional help, and if so, what kind of help?

These are three of the hundreds of common situations parents find themselves dealing with as their kids become teenagers. Inevitably the questions arise: "Should we be concerned? How concerned should we be? What should we do?" They range from incidents that are "to be expected," like the first time the sixteen-year-old gets a speeding ticket, to "never in our life did we think this could happen," like the phone call I got from Carly's parents after they saw the images she'd shared on Instagram. The advice they're likely to get ranges from "let them tough it out" to "bring in the experts, as this is a crisis." The problem is that, depending on who is giving them the advice, they can get either kind of answer.

When I get calls like these, there are certain variables I weigh carefully before I determine how concerned to be and in what direction to go. I am very clear with parents when I think they are expecting too much (like the dad who called me because he was concerned that his thirteen-year-old son "didn't have goals," was content getting a few Bs along with his As, and just wanted to hang out with his friends). In cases like his, I will guide the parents to relax, let their kid be a kid, be grateful that he is not doing anything dangerous, and point out that it would be rare to find a thirteen-year-old boy with well-defined goals beyond a desire to get to the highest level of a video game or to play basketball with his friends.

When I get calls like the one from thirteen-year-old Brooke's parents, who were concerned about the sudden collapse in her friend group, I want to know more. The two things Brooke will ultimately need to learn is how to find the right people to be friends with (something most adolescents will go through as they leave childhood behind) and how to not take things that aren't personal, personally. Depending on several factors in her temperament and personality, this will either be easier or harder to teach her to do. In this way, hard wiring and natural temperament matter and often a lot.

When Hard Wiring Makes
Life More Challenging

This is especially true for teens whose hard wiring does not make it especially easy for them to function and manage in our current fast-paced, highly competitive, high stimulation culture, even when they may appear to be fine.

Consider this perspective: The world we live in now is far easier to navigate and manage for people who like being around and engaging with lots of people a lot of the time, who are comfortable approaching and meeting new people, who are comfortable with competition and even drawn toward it, and who tend to easily let things roll off their backs. It becomes significantly more challenging when even one of those variables change. When all of them do, life can be almost agonizingly difficult.

Many of the teens I write about in this book are facing one or more of these challenges, particularly the sensitivity character trait, which is frequently ignored or under appreciated. Often, to the outside world they look like bright, engaged, confident teens who are going places in their lives. Indeed, many of them are academically highly accomplished and socially very engaged. But there is an inner life they struggle with because things do bother them, they're privately ruminating on life's deeper questions, and they rarely find anyone they can comfortably express this to, making it a difficult and sometimes very lonely time.

They are seeking more than the external markers of success. They commonly seek such things as relationships with people with whom they can feel authentic and deeply connected, work that feels meaningful and deeply satisfying, and engagement in substantive, thought-provoking dialogue with intelligent people. There is a time and place to play and be lighthearted and a time and place for more depth. Pop culture provides plenty of the former. Finding the rest and cultivating a life that provides the rest is where things get challenging.

Others face greater struggles because they do not possess two or more of these traits. Nowhere is this more painful for many parents to witness than when their teen struggles to connect and engage socially. Sometimes this is due to a lack of skills. Often, it is due to how hard it is to find the right peers to connect with, ones who share their values and level of commitment.

Though it may be easier to have those other traits, easier does not mean better. Indeed, many high-achieving leaders in all sorts of fields, from politics to science to arts to athletics to business, have been introverts, who are more sensitive and more intense, even eccentric. But again, eccentric is not bad ... it is just different enough from the norm to stand out.

None of these traits are all or nothing, black or white. All of them operate on a continuum. Some things can be changed. Others cannot. The work, then, becomes helping the adolescent on their journey to be the kind of person they are in a world that may not make that easy, as they navigate their own unique path in life. It is to accept that which is constant and will not change in them, while being willing to do what is necessary to change the things that can change and need to change.

Which leads me back to the case of Carly, the fifteen-and-a-half-year-old girl whose mom found her illicit pictures on her phone. Most of the time, parents handle this kind of behavior punitively. They give their teens lectures or punish them or both. The points they want to get across are about how risky these behaviors are and how this compromises their ability to trust their teen. The talks inevitably include how hard it is to regain trust once it has been lost. I often caution parents against "trusting" anyone before they are capable of trusting themselves. Most teens will tell parents with the best of intentions that they would not do what are clearly stupid things, but they say this before they've ever actually been in the situation in which they're required to resist both peer pressure and temptation— and say no.

By the time I speak to most parents in these situations, the lectures and grounding have already occurred, typically repeatedly. In spite of this, the behaviors have continued to happen. By that point, parents are seeking outside help, as a troubling situation has now become a troubling family problem. Rarely does any parent take action before these events have happened more than once. Carly's parents were different, though. They quickly got beyond their outrage at being lied to and embraced a much bigger and more comprehensive life question: *How can we best prepare our daughter for the peer world she is in, given who she is and the challenges she will face?* They knew their daughter well enough to know that she hadn't behaved in this way merely to satisfy her curiosity. Instead, out of insecurity, she was trying to impress her friends. If she was willing to go this far to do so at this age, how much further would she go down the line? With Carly, the work was to help her build her self-confidence and security, which would empower her to have healthier boundaries and make better decisions.

There are so many Carlys (and Carls, for that matter) out there— adolescents who need a significant boost in self-confidence to solidify their sense of self. These adolescents need more social skills, perspective, and savvy to navigate a tricky peer world, a pressure-filled academic world, and the complex, chaotic larger world they must be equipped to inhabit. Too often their "typical teen behaviors" are treated in isolation as "bad behavior" that needs to be punished, rather than as a wake-up call to parents that it is time to give their kids a different sort of education, one that requires a kind of teaching and learning that is not going to come from conventional schooling or more time spent grounded. My hope through the stories shared in this book is to inspire and equip more parents to seize this opportunity like Carly's parents did and offer their teens the guidance and life education now that will pay enormous dividends later.

> How can we best prepare our daughter for the peer world she is in, given who she is and the challenges she will face?

Often, if reached early enough, the same solutions can be applied to teens who are struggling in far more dramatic and concerning ways than Carly was, ways that often quickly get pathologized but don't actually need to be.

Such was the case with Leah.

chapter
three

From "I Don't Need This" to "I'm Glad I Met You": Leah, Her Parents, and a Journey to Adulthood

While ultimately her parents would work through their problems and save their marriage, there was a period of time when the future was really uncertain. This is when I met Leah.

Leah was in tenth grade and only fifteen years old when things hit rock bottom. Her grades had tanked, and one night her parents came home to find her stumbling drunk, alone in her bedroom with a bottle of vodka. She'd been hiding her self-medicating behavior for months. This wasn't a cry for help from Leah; rather, it was a shocking wake-up call to her parents that things were far more difficult for their daughter than they'd realized.

They'd already had meetings with the teachers at school and were tired of hearing the same old "she's really bright" and "if she would only apply herself." They had been seeing a family therapist for several months, and Leah had been seeing a psychotherapist on her own for four months, one whose specialty was adolescents. This therapist insisted there were "layers of work to do to get to the bottom of her issues" and that they were making progress, but Leah herself dismissed the process as "a waste of time and money." She explained that, from her perspective, "All she does is sit there and ask me what's going on and how I feel about this or how I feel about that. It's just stupid." Her parents, too, questioned whether any of this was making a difference. They reasoned that they could hire all the tutors in the world and work with a dozen therapists certified to work with adolescents, but if their daughter wasn't invested, or the method wasn't effective, or the practitioner wasn't the right person, then maybe Leah was right—maybe it was a waste of time and money.

They were in the throes of the great challenge any parent who has a struggling child face: finding help from someone whom they trusted with their child and who was also truly effective.

Leah's parents were professionally and financially successful. Leah's mother set a high bar. She was one of the most highly educated, accomplished people I've ever worked with. Renowned in her field, her innovations and breakthroughs had contributed to saving many lives, and she was regularly invited to speak at conferences around the world. They lived in a beautiful home in the hills with a stunning view of San Francisco Bay and the Golden Gate Bridge. Materially, they had everything. They also possessed two things even more valuable: progressive, open minds and a determination to find a solution, refusing to give up no matter what it took.

I often meet parents like Leah's after the conventional methodologies they've tried have proven ineffective. If just once in the three months they'd worked with the therapist their daughter had come home and said, "I like her, and I think this will help," they would have stuck with it. Instead, with one arm wrapped around her stumbling, drunk fifteen-year-old and the other one reaching for a towel to clean up the vomit, Leah's mom determined there had to be another way.

We had a long conversation over the phone about the journey they'd been on with Leah. She found a resonance in the description on my website about the difficult and often lonesome path of the more sensitive, thoughtful teen—and how, once they learn to put the pieces together, the life that opens up for them is extraordinary. "It really spoke to me when you said that part about how challenging it is to be a more thoughtful teen in today's society. It was as though you were describing my daughter," she told me. "I've felt all along like she is still a really good kid who is just struggling, yet all the teachers and counselors treat her like there is something wrong with her."

> If just once in the three months they'd worked with the therapist their daughter had come home and said, "I like her, and I think this will help," they would have stuck with it. Instead, with one arm wrapped around her stumbling, drunk fifteen-year-old and the other one reaching for a towel to clean up the vomit, Leah's mom determined there had to be another way.

A few days after I had that initial conversation with her mom, Leah stepped in the door to my old office on Clement Street in San Francisco. She was short with ginger hair, had braces, wore lots of makeup, and was definitely *not* happy to be there. Her skepticism wasn't something she hid either; she came right out with it.

"I'm not really sure why I am here. I keep telling them I don't need therapy. *They* are the ones who need it!" she announced boldly. I started laughing out loud when she said that. I laugh out loud a lot in my work, and often I have to teach my clients to remember how to do so, too—especially, to relearn how to do so without needing to be high on substances to find things funny or to let loose. It's sad to me how many people have lost touch with this side of themselves.

We spoke for almost an hour and a half. I learned that while her parents arguing stressed her out and worried her, the difficulty she had connecting with them was even more frustrating to her.

I learned that she'd had lots of friends until the end of seventh grade, when things began to change. She told me a long, convoluted story about a boy, jealousy, new cliques forming, and how a new girl moving into the school led to a split in her friend group, leaving her left out. High school began, and things only got worse. None of those girls would include her anymore.

She spent most of her time at school feeling lost and alone. The few peers she had who would spend lunch with her or do things with her on weekends were not the "cool" ones she used to associate with. Boys just wanted to use her for sex, often asking for handjobs and blowjobs even though they had no feelings for her. Her self-confidence had cratered. She had trouble focusing in school, was failing two classes, and had to go to summer school just to be able to move on to tenth grade.

The drinking had begun during the summer between her freshman and sophomore years in high school. By the time I met her, a month into her sophomore year, she was really lost, feeling very alone and utterly confused by how her social and academic life had declined so far since middle school.

"Things used to be so much easier. Everyone keeps giving me the same advice about 'just work hard' and telling me how smart I am. Then they say things that are supposed to make me feel better, like 'Don't take it personally' and 'Who cares what anyone thinks about you?' as if that is even possible. The therapist keeps wanting me to talk about how I feel, and it makes me feel like there is something wrong with me."

"Well, you're in luck," I quickly interject.

"Why do you say that?"

"Because I am never going to ask you how something makes you feel. I'm not going to convince you to get good grades. I will probably give you grief about drinking vodka straight up because I think that's just disgusting!" I said, with a grin and playful tone. Then I continued, "I may try to help you and your parents connect better. That is, of course, if you want me to. And the one thing I will definitely do is help you figure out what you want and how to get there, in spite of what's happened and in spite of what is happening. But the first thing is, you have to decide if you want to work with me because I won't work with you just because you are being told you have to see someone. You may struggle with schoolwork, and you may be struggling to figure out what in the world is going on with your peers, but you are not stupid. You need someone who will speak to you straight and someone who will challenge you and treat you like a teen becoming a young adult, not like you are a lost child."

"Yeah, but what if I feel like a lost child?" she asked.

"You won't for much longer," I replied confidently.

"That's kind of bold to say."

"It's not something I doubt that I can deliver," I replied. With her, I not only knew that I could help; I knew I'd already begun to. I also knew that projecting that kind of confidence was something she needed to begin undoing the damage done by all the doubt that had been conveyed by so many others.

She sat there for about thirty seconds, just staring at me, taking it in, trying to make sense of it. When she finally spoke, she looked me straight in the eyes and in the sincerest, most humble voice said, "It's strange. I feel like you hardly know me and I hardly know you, but at the same time, it's like you already know me..." Then after another long pause, she added earnestly, *"I'm really glad I've met you."*

We worked together regularly for the next two years, then more sporadically over the next few years after that. I watched her grow into maturity so quickly that she far surpassed many of her peers in self-confidence, direction, and social competence.

Leah is twenty-four now. In spite of her failing grades back in her first year of high school, she now holds a degree from the University of California at Santa Barbara. While it took her several years of mucking her way through various social groups as well as a few boyfriends (and a few "bad boys" along the way), she now has a full-time career and the solid support of true, loyal friends, and she awakens each day excited to be alive and on the adventure of her life.

I remember that first conversation with Leah where she said, "I'm glad I met you" like it was yesterday. It was in that exchange when I realized something that would become foundational in my work:

I realized that I saw these kids differently than their schools were seeing them and differently than their psychotherapists were seeing them. And I was offering them something very unique.

Whereas the school saw them as troubled (or just plain trouble) and the psychologists saw them as wounded and suffering from a psychological issue needing treatment, I saw them for the best of who they could be but just weren't yet. I saw in Leah a young girl who was loaded with potential to live a tremendously full life—a girl who was charming, sweet, thoughtful, intense, sensitive, and strong but who didn't recognize her own strengths and didn't yet have the skills to live that life. My work wasn't to fix her or heal her; it was to help her realize who she really was and to equip her with every skill she'd need to be the kind and quality of person she was, in a world that doesn't necessarily make it easy to be that person. In a way, you could say I was already about five years out in her future—at a time when she had already grown into this confident, flourishing young woman— so all that remained was to do the work necessary to get her there, too.

Now that I have led many "Leahs" on this journey, the model and the territory is very clear to me. How to actually get there is where the learning, challenge, and adventure always remains. One thing for certain is that far more often than not, psychotherapy is not the answer— and can even do more harm than good.

> Whereas the school saw them as troubled (or just plain trouble) and the psychologists saw them as wounded and suffering from a psychological issue needing treatment, I saw them for the best of who they could be but just weren't yet.

chapter
four

When Psychotherapy Is Not the Answer

*Psychotherapy theory turns it all on you: you are the one who is
wrong. But if a kid is having trouble or is discouraged, the problem
is not just inside the kid; it's also in the system, the society.*
—James Hillman

In the 1984 film *The Karate Kid*, Ralph Macchio plays a New
Jersey teenager who moves with his mother to Southern
California. Macchio doesn't fit in. As the new kid in his high school,
he finds himself bullied by a popular group of surfer boys who all

belong to the same karate school. Macchio's anger at being teased and humiliated compels him to pull a prank on the bullies that leads to him being severely beaten. He is saved by Mr. Miyagi, an old Karate master who takes Macchio under his wing and in a rather unorthodox way trains him in the ways of the martial arts, launching his self-confidence and personal discipline, all while instilling in him a deep sense of humanness and ethics about how to be a man of tremendous honor and character.

Today, they'd just send Macchio to counseling.

In *The Karate Kid*, Macchio's problems stem from his environment, from being an outsider attempting to fit into a world that rejects him not because he is socially inept or emotionally disturbed but for being from New Jersey. Parents whose teens are genuinely struggling with personal issues have a fundamental assessment and decision to make: Does their teen have "something wrong with them" requiring psychological and/or medical treatment from someone who treats psychopathology? Or is there something else going on that will be solved by addressing the "something else"? In this chapter, I lay out several considerations, including various alternative paths that often produce dramatic positive results. This discussion dares to walk the line of oversimplifying things that are quite complex, while avoiding the more contemporary tendency to make things more complex than they actually are.

When our young children get sick, we quickly learn to judge when an illness is severe enough to call for a doctor appointment, versus when just a day of rest and some chicken soup are needed. When they come to us in tears, we're able to gauge whether the problem is something we need to talk through with them, versus when a simple hug is enough. If only it were that simple when they become adolescents, and we watch them coping with the stress of coming of age in a complex, chaotic world. It's easy to understand why worried parents are ready to believe the worst. The best-seller lists and morning talk shows are populated with messages about what bad shape our kids are in. Whether it's the fragile, repressed inner lives of boys as they struggle to cope with meeting the dominant cultural one-dimensional, tough-guy archetypes of manhood, or the suffering of girls who struggle as much in relation to one another as they do with stereotypes imposed on them by pop culture and media, the picture they paint is bleak—and mostly overblown.

The good news is that, statistically, only a very small percentage of people actually have serious clinical depression or severe mental illness—around 3 percent. More commonly, episodes of feeling depressed are contextual, brought on by reactions to situations. The same is true of episodes of anxiety, the most commonly diagnosed mental illness. Typically, they will go away on their own, without intervention. Yet the lines "I think he's depressed" or "She suffers from anxiety" get used so casually and so frequently, it would seem that half the teen world is mentally ill!

> This discussion dares to walk the line of oversimplifying things that are quite complex, while avoiding the more contemporary tendency to make things more complex than they actually are.

While in my years of practice, I have seen many boys and girls who wrestle with these kinds of challenges (many examples of which I share in this book), I've rarely encountered one who is so damaged as to have developed a psychological disorder requiring clinical medical or psychological treatment. These are most often sociological issues, not psychological ones, yet the modern tendency is to overreact—to pathologize these natural, predictable stages in growing up, and to push kids into weekly therapy sessions or even onto medication. Too often, this is the wrong path, one that can actually do more harm than good.

> Yet the lines "I think he's depressed" or "She suffers from anxiety" get used so casually and so frequently, it would seem that half the teen world is mentally ill!

When to Seek Immediate Professional Help

Certainly, there are cases where a conventional clinical model, including medication, clinical psychological treatment, family therapy, or intensive inpatient treatment may be the best option available. Parents would be advised to seek professional psychological help when they are dealing with these serious mental health issues. Examples of this are kids who have issues such as serious substance addictions, violent tendencies, serious suicidal inclinations, persistent eating disorders, or other serious mental illnesses like clinical depression or personality disorders that make it difficult if not nearly impossible for them to function and relate in the conventional world. Families where there is a history of mental illness are often advised to be more alert to these showing up. Sadly, I have watched adolescents become mentally unstable after just one bad drug experience. This is more common with hallucinogenic drugs, though I have watched it happen with the accumulation of consistent use of lighter weight drugs like marijuana. Severe family dysfunction also frequently leads youth to destabilize as they become adolescents, and having a highly skilled family therapist work with a motivated family can make an enormous difference.

Far more often than not, though, these kinds of interventions are unnecessary in solving normal problems that can be dealt with in a healthier, less clinical way—and with much better results. Being "depressed" over a breakup, being moody going through puberty and hormonal changes, or feeling anxious about measuring up in school are not reasons to rush off to prescribe meds and receive psychological treatment. Most of these episodes are contextual and will fade in time. Often they can be addressed with good advice, a listening ear, exercise, a good night's sleep, and, sometimes, using lesser known approaches that are growing more common, as more progressive parents are doing.

> Far more often than not, though, these kinds of interventions are unnecessary in solving normal problems that can be dealt with in a healthier, less clinical way—and with much better results.

Consider these alternatives that can quickly solve many adolescent problems.

Integrative Health

Many progressive, more holistic, integrative doctors and thinkers cite the growing body of evidence that points toward many mood and regulation issues and disorders as having biological roots, stemming from toxicity and malnutrition, overexposure to EMFs, and/or understimulation brought on by things like too much screen time and not enough active movement—movement that is critical to learning and brain development in early ages. Many "disorders" have been cured simply by switching to the proper foods (especially eliminating bad food choices that cause digestive issues or brain inflammation), receiving proper vitamin and mineral supplementation, using probiotics to restore healthy bacteria to the digestive system, and/or retraining the nervous system through various movement therapies. None of those treatments are invasive or require anything manufactured by a pharmaceutical company. They are simple, wholesome, and effective. Anxieties, sleep problems, emotional regulation challenges, focus issues, and so on have all been shown to improve by living a healthier lifestyle and restoring healthy balance. Often the improvements are dramatic.

When the System Is the Source

Very often the source of the problem is actually the system in which the teens are being forced to function, rather than the teens themselves. This is the classic round peg / square hole dilemma. Most commonly this involves school pressure and/or the parents' own stress, expectations, and policies. By addressing these, we change their lives.

When we have become a culture that defines a "good" school as one where a child is most likely to get into Harvard and least likely to be jumped by a gang, we are missing the cost that comes from focusing too heavily on the "get into Harvard" part, and many schools become factories of stress for adolescents. The "one-size-fits-all" model of education only works well for those who fit that one size, which, in my observation, only about a third of students do. Remember the "one size" includes the ability to manage the social element as well as the academic, and typically one of these alone is enough to generate massive unrest in a person.

In contrast, I've had the privilege to work with a large number of summer camps and thousands of campers, parents, and camp professionals. I couldn't calculate the number of times I have heard the story about the child who has all sorts of issues at home and at school that require intensive treatment but who inexplicably thrives while at camp, needing none of that. The anxiety, insomnia, and depression all go away for a few magical weeks each summer.

Is it that the camp is the "magic pill" or is it that the school and/ or home system (including the distracting presence of electronics) is the source of the problem?

> I couldn't calculate the number of times I have heard the story about the child who has all sorts of issues at home and at school that require intensive treatment but who inexplicably thrives while at camp, needing none of that.

As much as it would be a marketing boon to camps, I don't think they're the magic pill. Instead they are the place where many common unhealthy forces aren't and where the context that brings out the best is. It's a remarkable formula for creating mental health.

Likewise, we have helped many teens resolve issues by doing things as simple as changing teachers, dropping a stress-inducing AP course, moving seats around in a classroom, rearranging a bedroom to provide more light or more quiet (including removing the TV), and providing tutors. Sometimes the changes made are more dramatic, like switching majors, changing schools, or leaving school altogether.

Many teens do much better at a smaller school, with smaller classes that employ a more customized approach to learning. Increasingly, progressive schools are establishing a variety of "schools within a school," often with focused programs that allow a portion of each day to be spent immersed in doing and learning things that generate immediate pleasure, like creating films, studying applied science, or participating in active "day trading" investing projects. These kinds of programs also enable teachers to have more personalized relationships with their classes. That connection alone is often calming and enough to make an enormous difference. Some high schools are starting school later to accommodate teen sleep patterns and, like Japan, are limiting homework to avoid burnout and to maximize retention. I often advise parents to familiarize themselves with the resources and options available, as well as to win over the influencers in their child's school. Getting the right teachers and the right schedule can go a long way to relieve stress, eliminating the symptoms of things like anxiety and depression.

At home, parents giving their teen more "freedom" and/or opportunities for more real challenges and responsibilities can make an enormous difference. This includes all sorts of variations of learning to communicate better with their teen and better supporting their true deeper needs, including providing more opportunity to do activities that generate real joy.

When They Do Need Someone to Talk To

The most prominent and readily available forms of "talk" intervention in our culture are counseling and psychotherapy. Counseling is more of a problem-solving model, while psychotherapy is done by licensed clinical psychologists and is designed to treat psychological disorders. Few parents possess a substantive understanding of the different psychotherapeutic models or the beliefs they orient from. In the eyes of the general public, a psychologist is a psychologist, in the same way a pediatrician is a pediatrician. This is simply not the case.

Psychotherapists assess how certain behaviors relate to someone having a mental disorder and are trained to diagnose psychopathology—mental disorders in the form of mental illness or psychological disorders. They then treat these mental illnesses and psychological disorders. They do this by entering into a clinical relationship where they offer psychological treatment to their patient in the form of psychotherapy to help them heal from deep-seated mental issues, feelings, and destructive, unhealthy patterns in their lives.

The field of psychotherapy has evolved considerably since the days when Freud encouraged his patients to sit on a couch and talk freely about their dreams and their mothers, though the roots of his psychoanalytic model still influence modern practices, and those types of practitioners still exist today. In the last fifty years the humanistic, cognitive behavioral, family systems, brief therapy, and transpersonal movements have gained in popularity. Each of these has its variations and subcategories. Explaining the specifics of these different theories and methods is beyond the scope of this book.

The only concrete things that bind those trained and licensed in the psychotherapy field together are the requirements that they understand and can correctly implement the Diagnostic Statistical Manual (the guidebook of diagnosable mental disorders), which is something that both their license and insurance companies require and the confidentiality and mandatory reporting laws their state demands they adhere to. Based on their theoretical and clinical orientation, though, how they think about what is causing the issue a patient brings to them and what they do to treat the diagnosis can vary greatly.

With the exception of newer treatment models like the fast growing field of cognitive behavioral psychology, which directly teaches people new thinking and behavioral patterns and coping skills designed to make their lives more immediately functional (and is proving to be the most effective form of therapy for treating anxiety), most psychotherapy still focuses on delivering a patient several things: An emotionally safe place to talk confidentially, insights into their lives, and/or an opportunity to feel and express their emotions, as this is believed to be part of the healing process. While characters like the one Robin Williams played in *Good Will Hunting* offer an exciting persona for a clinical psychologist, in reality the vast majority of psychotherapists maintain a clinical, warm, yet impersonal distance in the relationship. They believe that keeping their own emotions and life story out of the room is essential for the patient to explore their own life story. In this way, the psychotherapist's job is to guide their patients on a journey of self-discovery, reconnecting with themselves, healing from past wounds, and ideally finding a new way to cope with life's challenges.

When Psychotherapy Works

Many people who do not have serious mental illnesses still find value in participating in psychotherapy. Most of the people I've met in my life who found great value in the psychotherapeutic process were adults, though, not teenagers.

Many of these adults appreciated the opportunity to talk about their problems to a nonjudgmental third party, including the guidance and help to learn to express themselves better. They appreciated the questions their therapist asked that helped them gain insight into their lives, allowing them to develop a theory explaining why they are the way they are. Others appreciated and found value in the opportunity the therapeutic process gave them to reconnect with their inner emotional life and the safe space to express these emotions.

These adults were able to extrapolate practical value from this, ensuring that these weren't just fifty-minute gripe sessions where they went to vent but not actually make changes. They were cognitively advanced and life experienced enough to know that while venting may feel good, it doesn't make things change. They were able to find a way to take these insights and experiences and translate them into useful change in behaviors or beliefs.

Rarely do these processes produce the same results and satisfaction for adolescents, though. Many psychotherapists have confided in me how they have stretched the boundaries of their training in an attempt to work effectively with adolescents. There are limits to how far they can go, though, and this often contributes to the limits of their effectiveness. In contrast, with the Evolution Mentoring model, I regularly take calls from clients late at night, meet them for lunch, talk to their parents, and once even took a seventeen-year-old with me to a program I was running in London, a story I will share later. It's just radically different to be this available and this proactive and not being limited by having to keep my own opinions and life out of the room.

From *The Karate Kid* to a Clinical Case: What If Macchio Had Been Sent to a Psychotherapist Instead of a Sensei?

Macchio was fortunate that the story of *The Karate Kid* took place in 1984. Today, as a young adolescent, Macchio would have been sent to his school counselor, who would have called his mother in for a meeting, expressed concern about him, and then referred him to a psychologist specializing in adolescents, who would have begun weekly fifty-minute sessions with him.

Macchio would have been identified as having anger issues, most likely with an attachment disorder and depression, which they determined stemmed from his father having abandoned him. Macchio and the psychologist would have spent time in these psychotherapy sessions exploring his "issues." Macchio would've talked about how it felt to be all alone with no friends at school, how it felt not to have his father in his life, and how it felt to be the butt of jokes and constantly emasculated by the bullies at school. The sessions would have focused a lot of attention on the hardships and sadness that must have come from the father abandonment, as well as the connection between his feeling emasculated and his father's absence. They would have gone in depth to help him access the deep wounds of anger this caused him and the sadness beneath it. The sessions would have been intense, and even if he wasn't struggling with any of these things, the psychologist would have likely tried to convince him that he was and that going into the pain was his only hope. *Kind of depressing, isn't it?*

But that is not what happened to Macchio's character.

Instead, he met a masterful, wise old man who saw him not as psychologically ill, emotionally scarred, and in need of treatment but as a young boy with a heart of gold who had the potential to achieve greatness. A man who was willing to take him under his wing, show him the way, and guide him to mastery … and all without ever once asking how he felt or even caring how he felt.

This is more than just the stuff of fairy tale Hollywood movies. It is possible in real life. This book is based on it.

Why It's Different with Adolescents

I often receive calls from parents who have tried psychotherapy for their struggling teen and found it to be ineffective. So when I get the phone call—countless times now in my career—that begins with "We've had our son in therapy, and nothing seems to be changing," I say, "We should probably talk."

My experience is that most adolescents don't want or need psychological treatment, because there isn't anything wrong with them. What they suffer from are not mental illness issues; they are growing up issues. What they need is an education in life.

Just think about the context. Most adolescents are already feeling vulnerable enough, so the last thing they want to do is talk to a stranger about scary, painful things. They certainly don't want to be treated like a "patient," because that presupposes they are ill. While there are many highly skilled therapists out there who are capable of building substantial rapport with teens, there is still the very relevant matter of whether or not a teen has the maturity to utilize the process to find value in it. In general, they don't have the maturity or sophistication to be able to turn insights into action or even to generate the motivation to do so. What they need is guidance and training, not talking about feelings.

Perhaps most importantly, they often don't have enough life experience to be able to discern what is useful input and what is not, what to believe and what to reject. Because of this, a therapist—especially the more conventional classically trained one—is actually in a position to offer them input and ideas that can be destabilizing, taking what seemed like normal teen insecurities that stem from not yet having acquired the requisite skill set needed in each stage of development and making it seem like their mother or father or other life circumstances are to blame for it. That often leaves them wondering what else might be wrong with them because of their upbringing, making them feel even less in control. I've seen this happen too many times to ignore the dangers of it.

A frustration that parents who've had their child in psychotherapy also commonly express to me is with the sense of secrecy between the clinician and their child regarding what is being talked about and how hard it is to get a straight answer when they inquire about progress or when they ask for advice regarding things going on at home. What many parents really need, they come to realize, is not someone to "fix" their child but rather someone to partner with them in helping them raise their child in a complicated and confusing stage of life. Yes, their child needs help, but so do they.

Understanding why things happen and knowing what to do about it are not enough.

So much of the emphasis in conventional counseling and psychotherapy is placed on understanding "Why?" Why do I feel the way I do? Why do I feel like I am not as good as others? A lot of emphasis is also placed on how these things make a person feel.

Understanding why things happen and being able to express how it makes a person feel may be useful for adults who are far more cognitively advanced and complex, and it may comfort the curious, but functionally it holds little to no value unless it leads to action that produces results.

Similarly, just knowing what to do to get results is also rarely enough. People also have to be able to actually do what is needed to get the results. This means they must have the skills, confidence, attitude, discipline, and capacity to take action, even when it won't be easy and won't feel good.

If the example of *The Karate Kid* does nothing else, it dramatizes the extent that excellent training, coaching, and mentoring can help a person to learn, grow, and evolve, often much quicker than they would ever do on their own and certainly in ways they would never do if they spent that same time in a room talking about how bad they felt and what bad thing happened that week.

These are some of the reasons I made the decision very early in my career to steer away from the conventional clinical psychological approaches to helping adolescents and to focus instead on creating something that is far more comprehensive, that often offers something far deeper and greater in scope and impact, for both the adolescents and their parents. Rather than reinvent the wheel, I realized I needed to update it—by revisiting and reimagining one of the most powerful roles in human society, that of the wise mentor.

Third Voice™—Not Parent, Not Friend

GREAT ADVICE, WRONG SOURCE

Not infrequently with adolescents, I see this phenomenon: Their parent gives them great advice, but because it comes from their parent they discard it. Yet, if it came from someone else, they would embrace it. "Great advice, wrong source" is something one of my client's grandmothers used to say. I think that line is brilliant and very wise. Parents can have tremendous credibility to a teen, but other factors may make the teen reject their words. Often parents' emotional attachment impedes their ability to be objective about the challenges their teens experience. Advice they might freely and comfortably give to someone else's teen, they sometimes struggle to give to their own. Parents also have the real and symbolic role of representing dependence, at the stage when a young person is in need of establishing his or her independence. Parents' expectations often hold such gravitas in a teen's mind that hearing criticism can be especially difficult when it comes from them. Because of this, even when parents give great advice, it can get rejected.

It Takes Three

When I first started my private practice and explained what I would be offering their son, a father said to me: "It takes three." He explained how a professor in college had taught him that it takes at least three adult relationships to help raise a child into adulthood, parents offering just one. I couldn't agree more; I'd go further and say it even takes more than three, but three of the right ones can be enough. Before we even had children, my wife and I began "collecting" responsible adults we wanted in our children's lives. We know that the time will come when our children either won't want to hear it from us or will just want other opinions. How invaluable it will be for them to have responsible adults they can turn to rather than just their peers, who know as little about life as they do.

If you are a parent, as you read through the many anecdotes I share in this book, I encourage you to think about how you can bring adults (young and older) into your sons' and daughters' lives who can offer them similar kinds of learning, coaching, training, and guidance. Ideally these should be people who are proactive, positive, and willing to be available to your son or daughter—people who fulfill what I call being a Third Voice (the family is the first voice, peers and pop culture are the second voice, and the wise, experienced expert is the Third Voice). The old African proverb "It takes a village" may be the most universal piece of wisdom ever spoken.

The most influential and helpful mentors and guides for me growing up were mostly just deeply kind people who happened to also have a whole lot to teach me about how life works. They were also people who were willing to go over and above to be available and even to take the lead to teach me things I would one day need to know. They saw my potential and contributed to me realizing it.

Two of the most significant were my paternal grandfather, Ben Leiken, and a family friend and peer of my parents, Patsy Rubin.

My grandfather taught me through his endless stories and his consistent, congruent modeling. His was the classic immigrant success story—the first in our family line to go to university, who went on to a sixty-year career as a lawyer. He prided himself on always being honest, honorable, and generous. At his funeral, an elderly client of his made it a point to come to me and tell me a story about how my grandfather once forgave his debt in exchange for a bushel of corn because that was all he could afford at the time. If it were an isolated story, it would be one thing. That it was just one of many stories about his integrity and generosity, many of which I witnessed, only furthered the impact that having him so present in my childhood and coming of age had on me. Through this relationship I learned the value of the wise elder, the storyteller, as well as the irreplaceable impact of just being able to spend time in the presence of someone who modeled such an elegant and positive way of life.

> The most influential and helpful mentors and guides for me growing up were mostly just deeply kind people who happened to also have a whole lot to teach me about how life works.

Patsy Rubin was the rare adult who knew how to connect with kids of all ages, including teenagers. Numerous times I would call her or literally just show up at her home unannounced, seeking advice and reassurance that only she could provide—and she never failed to give it. What I loved about the way she offered it was that whatever advice she gave was practical, specific, and doable. And no matter how down and discouraged I was, she always made me feel like I was really okay and that there was always hope. Patsy wouldn't let me spend my time in tears, though I tried. She would quickly turn them into seeds for laughter. It was rare as a teen to find an adult who gave advice that was more than just generalities and clichés. From Patsy I learned how to do this and to always instill hope.

It was in those relationships, and later when I became a staff member at summer camp and got to be in that role for others, that

I realized the power of being in a role that is neither parent nor friend. I learned from summer camp that there is a great leverage and opportunity in playing the Third Voice, the in-between role in a child's life. Though it took me many years to learn the boundaries and develop the model fully, in many ways what I have become is a professional camp counselor: cool, funny, playful, commanding, challenging, practical, wise, available, and most importantly, effective at getting results.

Finding adults who will be this for your sons and daughters may be the most valuable investment you can make for them. Unfortunately, our current culture does little to support this happening. It will likely require you as a parent to be proactive, asking friends, colleagues, and family to go over and above.

As becomes clear in the anecdotes in the remainder of this book, the relationship and way I work with adolescents that contributes to my getting these kinds of results is far outside the box. I believe in being transparent, authentic, and accessible to adolescents. Thus while there is sophisticated intention in the way I relate to the teens and young adults I work with, to the outside observer it will appear anything but formal, rigid, and clinical. But to the teen or young adult client, the relationship feels undeniably real.

My clients can call or text me twenty-four hours a day and will get responses, time, and input from me as they need it. Sure, I turn my ringer off at night, but being available to offer advice while they are still at the party where they just had a fight with their girlfriend or during lunch break as they are stressed out about an upcoming exam is far more valuable to them than having to wait until a week from Tuesday for their regularly scheduled appointment. It also allows me to have clients all over the world, to be proactive, and to be just as available to give advice and input to parents.

In contrast to conventional psychotherapy, I also believe that focusing on bad feelings and dwelling on memories of negative events is counter-productive and should be avoided. It's not to deny that these things happened; it's more to ensure that clients don't feed the memories and give them even more time and energy to impede their own growth. My bias is to learn from these mistakes and setbacks and move forward quickly, no matter how painful they were. The same is true for bad moods and bad feelings. I don't give them unneeded attention, as they are transitory. Often the bad mood is actually what is causing the problem. Rather than spend lots of time dwelling on inhibitory stories about events, I guide clients into a most balanced and positive state, where suddenly they feel like more is possible and they have a sense of personal control and power again. Then, when they are feeling at ease and possess a sense of possibility, I ask my clients to tell me what it is they want. This may sound simple, but the simplicity of it can be deceiving. What comes from this is actually profoundly useful.

Inevitably the answers they give point to wanting things like the following:

- They want to be more confident.

- They want to be able to get themselves to take action and produce results, in spite of how challenging it may be to do so.

- They want to know themselves well enough to be certain they are making the best choices for themselves.

- They want to be socially skilled, savvy, and sophisticated.

- They want to become more discerning in their relationship choices (e.g., to be able to read people better and be much better judges of character).

- They want to become more savvy and adept at navigating their way through various institutions and systems.

- They want to become more disciplined, overcoming the temptations for immediate gratification and instead developing the habits and work ethic that lead to excellence.

Notice that everything on this list is positive. *What they realize is that when they have these things, things that were bothering them or inhibiting them no longer will.*

Gaining these skills, attributes, character traits, and mind-sets is not a healing process. It is a learning and growing process.

To truly evolve and transform into an adult requires things like learning new skills, stepping outside of one's comfort zone, practice, repetition, learning from mistakes, and taking action even when it isn't going to be easy to do and doesn't feel good.

One thing that is certain for adolescents is that getting excellent guidance, training, coaching, and mentoring can make an enormous difference, both in the quality of their growth and the speed at which it happens.

Finding the messengers is up to you.

The rest of this book helps clarify what the messages need to be.

PART TWO

THE THREE STAGES OF ADOLESCENCE
WHAT'S GOING ON,
WHY & HOW TO TRULY HELP

chapter
five

Crossing the First Bridge: Social Puberty
"Am I Cool Enough?"

"Mom, stop! I'm not a little kid anymore!"

Until the summer before eighth grade, Christopher was a sweet, compliant, fun-loving boy. He hung out with the neighborhood kids, threw a baseball in the yard with his dad, got good grades in school, and, except for some typical squabbles with his younger sister, pretty much got along with everyone. That summer, though, something radical happened.

He'd always been an early riser—but suddenly he wasn't waking up until ten. He was in the throes of puberty, having gained three inches and two shoe sizes in just a few months. His parents understood the need for sleep; they'd been teens once themselves. But then came the arguing about screen time. He'd never put up a fight before when told to turn the TV off. Now it was almost constant.

When school began, his mom's questions about homework were met with intense disdain and warnings to back off and leave him alone to do it himself. "I'm not a little kid anymore!" he frequently snapped.

It was a line his parents would hear repeatedly that year.

They quickly learned that Christopher's "not being a little kid anymore" also included lying about having his homework done, hiding his progress report when it was sent home (which was only sent home if there was a C or lower grade, of which he had two), and sneaking his phone into his room late at night so he could keep up with text exchanges with all his friends in school. When they took the phone away at one point because of his missing homework assignments and the detentions he got in school for "excessive socialization" and talking back to his teacher, you would have thought they'd taken away his manhood. He went ballistic, screaming at the top of his lungs, cursing, and eventually kicking a door.

The school psychologist suggested that he needed to "see someone," both for his addiction to his phone and for what was very likely the beginning stages of oppositional defiant disorder and potentially an anxiety disorder. She expressed concern about his "following the wrong crowd" and warned about how these things get out of control quickly. His parents' jaws dropped when this expert suggested that Christopher had some serious problems that needed psychological intervention. He was just turning fourteen, and only six months earlier everything had seemed fine.

Feeling deeply troubled, his mom picked up his phone and began to read the text messages between Christopher and his friends. Most of it was "Hey what's up?" and "Who do you like?"—typical of the notes her generation used to pass in school at his age. Then she saw some messages that disturbed her. One was about a boy on his Little League team who had stolen two bottles of Jack Daniels from the local supermarket, then invited a whole group of boys and girls over to get drunk with him. Another was about a boy whose older brother had given him weed and let him get high with him.

Though Christopher himself had not participated, he did act like he thought it was cool. He even offered to help one boy cover a lie by saying he'd been with him when really the boy was at the house party getting drunk.

His parents quickly saw where this was going. When they called Christopher into the room and confronted him with the news from his phone, he suddenly broke down in tears. Instead of seeing this monster with oppositional defiance, they saw a young boy who was in over his head. *He didn't need psychological help. He needed life help.*

"I heard you speak five years ago at our elementary school, and I kept your card," his mom explained when we had our first phone conversation. "We didn't need your help then, but boy, do we now." When she told me the story of what had gone on since last summer, I heard in her voice the echoes of a hundred other such conversations I've had with parents of young teens. The stories either go like Christopher's, where the teen is overwhelmed with the pressures and complications of keeping up socially, or where the teen is discouraged by what is not happening socially. For those other teens, the friends who used to call and include them no longer do. Their struggle is around the loneliness of having too little social contact.

Sure, I hear about the video games that have become a problem and the "It's only eighth grade, so grades don't really matter" struggles parents have motivating young teens to take school seriously (especially boys), but far and away the greatest source of stress at this age is trying to keep up, fit in, and navigate the complicated, confusing social world of the young teen.

Social Puberty

We all know how children go through physical puberty. Physical puberty is marked by things like growth spurts, getting acne, growing pubic hair, voices changing, girls getting breasts and menstruating, and all the hormonal changes and mood swings that come with them. It is tangible. But their social life goes through a puberty of its own that's less easy to spot.

Social puberty is intangible, but the invisible weight of it lies heavy on the life of young teens. It is also the driving force of the first stage of the teen years. With the adults in their lives, they are trying to establish "I am not a kid anymore" by proving they can do things on their own. Inside themselves, in relation to their peers, they are also trying to prove that they are "not a little kid anymore." This driving question they are trying to answer is "Am I cool enough?" The focus becomes almost single-mindedly on "Where do I fit in in the world of my peers?"

The disconnect between many parents, who easily get concerned about grades and how their son or daughter is ever going to get into college and get a job one day, and the young teen, who is consumed with where they fit in with the small world of their peer group now, couldn't be much greater. The help young teens need, ironically, couldn't be much easier to provide, if only the adults around them would see it, get it, and offer it.

Think about all the things going on in the young teen: It is in this stage of social puberty where sexuality awakens, as does the desire to connect sexually and romantically. The intensity of feelings makes the bonding and separating of couples more consuming. The happiness of watching friends fall head over heals for someone often turns to frustration as that same friend no longer has time for them since becoming consumed with their newfound love. This is when the chasm emerges between those who are "into" the other sex and those who are far from ready for that world. In this stage, social hierarchies develop, as does the acute awareness of what it feels like to be on the bottom looking up, and how hard and exhausting it is to stay up high (which, by the way, is where Christopher was and what consumed him). Typically, the most vicious of all social challenges that happens at this age is the extreme jealousy that emerges, typically between girls. Those who are inclined to be vindictive can do horrifically cruel things. Those who are not adept at handling conflict can be devastated and feel powerless. I cannot tell you how many calls I have received from parents of middle school girls over the years that begin with "My daughter comes home from school and cries almost every day."

> If social puberty is hard on young teens, it can be just as hard on their parents.

In this stage, cliques become dramatically divisive. Everyone knows who are the "stoners," who are the "popular kids," and who are the "theater kids," and other than rubbing elbows in class in school, rarely do they interact outside their circles. That divisiveness is one of the hardest things for young teens to come to terms with because often classmates who were once their best friends now belong to a completely different social circle, or worse, a completely different social hierarchy.

This is hard for parents, too, because often the parents of these kids are friends with one another, having bonded over gymnastics classes, soccer practices, school events, and sleepovers in the elementary school years. Now, they cannot just have family get-togethers anymore, because their kids are no longer friends. If social puberty is hard on young teens, it can be just as hard on their parents.

Lindsey's Mom Finds Her Allies

Lindsey was fourteen and a half and barely a month into high school when I first met her. Her mom reached out to me one afternoon, trusting a gut instinct that her daughter would need someone she could turn to for advice and guidance as she navigated the complex terrain of the teen years. While she had a super close relationship with her daughter, she also knew that it had been many years since she was a teen and that the world is vastly different now. She'd always be happy to give her daughter her opinion and advice but would rather Lindsey got it from someone who has some expertise in the teen social world.

At surface level there were no major problems with Lindsey. She got excellent grades in school, had lots of friends, was physically active, and, even though her parents were divorced and her dad lived on the other side of the state, she was remarkably well adjusted. As her mom knew, though, Lindsey was also the kind of person who tended to overanalyze things and who was highly sensitive. Everything, from certain foods to injustices in the world, caused distress to Lindsey. In her family she played the role of "peace maker" whenever her mom and older sister got into conflicts. Under stress, she would often get bad headaches; missing school because of them only made her more stressed.

Because of how composed she was outwardly, she was the kind of teen, like many of the teens I work with, whose friends were surprised she "talks" to someone. Her mom knew that Lindsey was going to have a lot of social distractions. From the minute I met her, I understood why. She was a beautiful girl with long dark hair, a bright smile, and tons of charisma and charm. Our first conversation involved her telling me about no less than eight of her "best friends" and three layers of drama involving each one of them. She was outgoing and an extrovert, and for anyone parenting a teen, be alert about that combination because you can be most certain your teen has a very busy social life ahead. These character trait/personality types are often misunderstood, yet they are a really important part of understanding what is going on with your teen during these early teen years.

An extrovert is a person who draws energy from being with people and often prefers to be around people a lot of the time. Extroverts get restless if they spend too much time alone. In contrast, introverts prefer being around a few people, often finding satisfaction in having just a few close friends. They tend to want and need more quiet or "down" time to recharge and find balance.

Outgoing people are at ease with and often excited by the prospects of talking to new people. Shy people tend to be tentative about speaking up in groups or approaching new people; they find the process tiring and may even fear those situations.

Another piece that's widely misunderstood is that these character and personality traits operate on a continuum. If "100" is the world's most extroverted person who can never get enough of being with people, being in crowds, and having endless social stimulation, then "1" is the world's most introverted person who lives in solitude, alone in a cave somewhere. Everyone else, including you, me, and your teens, are somewhere in between.

On that kind of scale, a girl like Lindsey is well in the seventies to eighties on both the extrovert and outgoing scale. It is no surprise that when Lindsey went to college, she immediately joined one of the most socially active sororities on campus. That's what highly extrovert/highly outgoing people do.

A boy like Christopher is actually far more outgoing than he is extroverted. It is easy for him to engage with others, but too much of it was taking a toll on him. He needed to learn how to pace his social life better.

Leah, the girl I began this book telling you about, was a classic case of a moderate introvert who was also somewhere around the midpoint in the shy/outgoing scale. This presented all sorts of challenges, as she was continually overdoing it socially and stressing herself to try and keep up.

But for Lindsey, socializing was not only easy, it was an enormous part of her life, so much so that when one of her many "best" friends proposed that they have a party at the house of one of the other girls when her parents were going to be out of town for the weekend, Lindsey went all in. Each of the girls came up with a story about where they were staying that night, and each of their parents believed it. Having not yet been initiated into the troubles of teens, parties, and how crazy it gets when a text message gets out there, they had no reason to worry. These were all "good kids with good heads on their shoulders," their parents thought.

And it's true—they were. But they were also teens in the throes of the first stage of teen life. "I'm not a kid anymore" comes with all sorts of behaviors attached. One of the most common of these is doing the things they perceive teenagers do, like drink, smoke, sneak out at night, "hook up," and, yes, throw parties. Unfortunately for these eight best friends, the eight boys they invited decided to tell a few other people. And they told a few people ... and by 9 o'clock at night, there were over a hundred high schoolers partying away at her friend's house. There was alcohol, drugs, people naked in the hot tub, and a whole bunch of upperclassmen who decided to show up.

One of them was a senior boy who played on the football team, was about 6'3", 230 pounds, drunk, loud, and towering over young Lindsey. It turns out that in his drunken state, he decided to tell her that he had been checking her out and wanted to "get with" her.

"What's up? I've seen you around campus. We should hang out. What's your number?"

Scared and overwhelmed, Lindsey tried to get away, but this towering, tough older boy followed her, continuing to ask for her number, each time getting more agitated that she wouldn't comply. Finally, he had her in a corner of a room, refusing to let her go until she gave it to him. She was on the verge of tears when her friends found her and pulled her away from him. The girls then all left the house and the wild party that they had started. Moments later the police showed up, and teens were jumping into the woods, running down the street. Over $10,000 of damage was done to the girl's house that night. Lindsey and the girls all slept at another girl's house, too scared to tell their parents, too drunk to go anywhere else.

When her mom found out about the party the next day, she went ballistic. She was lied to and deceived, and she was intent on grounding Lindsey until junior year! Hearing about the senior boy only reinforced the worst fear of most parents of girls, especially the extroverted, outgoing, charismatic, flirty ones like Lindsey.

But rather than ground her indefinitely, Lindsey's mom came up with a different plan.

She invited the parents of each of her friends to come meet at her home with the intention of mutually agreeing on rules, guidelines, and communication between them to ensure the girls were safe. She figured that with all the parents on board, an event like this couldn't happen again.

She was probably right: with all the parents on board, it probably couldn't happen again. But that is the problem; it takes everyone being aligned in their beliefs and expectations, and their commitment to uphold them, and that is really hard to come by, especially in today's world, where there is no unifying guiding moral force to take the place once held by religious faiths.

She called to tell me of her great idea and asked if I had any suggestions on what to bring up at the meeting of the parents.

I told her I had only one suggestion: "Go into this meeting with all these parents with only one goal in mind—to figure out who are your allies. That's it. Don't be surprised to find out that some of these parents have totally different values than yours. They'll say things like 'If they are going to drink, I'd rather they do it in my house.' Or 'I was smoking so much dope when I was their age, I'm not worried about it.' You just need to find the ones who want the same thing as you, so you'll know that when they are involved in your daughter's plans, you can sleep well at night."

The next night, her mom called me up. Indeed, she was shocked at the array of attitudes and beliefs these parents held. Only two others shared her belief that these fourteen- and fifteen-year-old girls were too young to be doing these things, needed a strict curfew, and needed to be more closely watched.

From the Inside Out

Lindsey and her mom had their moments of disagreement over the years, but to this day Lindsey respects her mom a hundred times over for standing by her principles, for being firm when it was needed, and for loosening up when the time came, a year and half later, that she was ready for it. I have so many other stories of teens who, looking back on it, feel the same way about parents brave enough to take the kind of stand Lindsey's mother took.

Teens—especially young teens in this "Am I cool enough?" stage of their journey from childhood into adulthood—do not need their parents to be their friends. The last thing they need is one more friend relationship to navigate through!

They do need to have adults in their lives who see them as cool enough and capable enough and as totally loveable. They need it from us, so that even in those times when it seems like no one else feels that way about them, they can know that someone does. They need the reassurance that someone who knows better than them, knows something for certain that they very much want to know, too, but don't yet.

There is something profound in that truth. It really matters. I have seen it repeatedly in my work.

I have seen the teens whose parents overtly or inadvertently send the message that they are not good enough and that their future may be in peril and the toll this takes on their teen. And I have seen the parents who even through all the strife and struggle that can happen during these years, consistently believe in their teen and see the best in them, even when they aren't displaying it—who are able to project confidence and security toward them, even when their teens are not feeling it themselves. I have seen teachers who can do it and how students who respect no one else, respect them.

I have played that role for so many of my clients over the years. "You can borrow some of my faith and confidence in you," I have said on a few occasions. "Believe me, I have more than enough for both of us!"

It is rarely something parents say because it's hard to speak it; so often the words sound clichéd and get the response "You are just saying that because you're my parent" or "Yeah, thanks." It must be something they feel when they're with you—literally something that is palpable in such a way that the force of your belief in their inherent goodness, worth, and value is so potent, they cannot help but feel better about themselves and about life when they are in your presence.

Many adults do not convey this with near enough intensity. Often this is because they are too distracted or get too focused on what their child is not doing, rather than on what they are.

Teens at this stage need us to keep our attention on building them up and on what they are doing right, not to ignore their flaws, but not to fixate on them either. They quickly "tune out" anything that sounds like lectures and clichés, but they perk up when something comes up at them with charisma and practical implications.

Because of this, my own approach is to be opinionated, outspoken, poetic, charismatic, funny, outlandish, forceful, metaphoric, direct, or whatever I need to be to help these young people on the verge of launching into adulthood to return once again to the place inside themselves where they feel whole, complete, and connected … and then from this place inside, begin to make decisions about what to be doing, where to be doing it, and who to be doing it with. I encourage you to be, too.

> It must be something they feel when they're with you—literally something that is palpable in such a way that the force of your belief in their inherent goodness, worth, and value is so potent, they cannot help but feel better about themselves and about life when they are in your presence.

For today's teens, when they interact with the adults in their lives, this is too rarely the case.

Let's change that.

chapter
six

Social Isolation, Exclusion, and Parenting Decisions

Many teens are on the other end of the social spectrum from a girl like Lindsey. Rather than having too many friends and too much happening too quickly, they have very few friends or too little social challenge. Sometimes it's because they have other interests; teens driven by intellectual pursuits or performance-related endeavors are often on their own track. Whether due to so few others sharing these interests or just the time demands required to pursue excellence, they may spend far less time with others their own age, if any one at all. This is not necessarily concerning, though to a certain extent it does delay their social and interpersonal development.

Addiction to technological stimulation is leading a growing number of young teens to disengage with peers, costing them enormous losses in development. While they often gain something through their virtual online community, there is a whole other level of learning to engage with in the real world that they are missing out on. Very often I find that if we meet these teens before it is too late, they are easily engaged and redirected outward. I've said to more than a few teen boys, "Which would you prefer, porn or the real thing?" After they blush and laugh nervously, they quickly agree it is time to start learning to live out here.

Far and away the most common cases of minimal social contact are more like the stories I will tell here. Meet Kenneth, Nick, and Jenny—three "great kids" who are struggling to connect even though they very much want to and for all intents and purposes should be.

Stories like theirs are far too common today.

Every Great Virtue, So Where Are the Friends: The Least-Texted Phone in School

The open gym night at the local rec center echoed with the sounds of teen boys playing basketball, spurring each other on with a constant barrage of the insults and one-upmanship that teen boys use to establish hierarchy: "Pass the ball, fags!" … "C'mon, don't be a pussy."… "Yo, Theo, sorry I'm late, but I was busy with your mom!" all being shouted over the sounds of sneakers squeaking and basketballs bouncing on the court.

As Kenneth's mom stood in the doorway, waiting for him to finish this last pickup game, she was appalled at the way these boys talked. She'd known many of these boys since they were in kindergarten. Several were boys she regularly drove in carpool. Today was one of those days.

When Theo and Michael got in the car for their ride home, she was amazed at how quickly they reverted to being polite, well-behaved boys. "Hi, Mrs. T!" they said as they got in the backseat, tossing their stinky basketball clothes in the back of her SUV. More upsetting to her, though, was the way they talked to each other about meeting with a few others later that night to go see the new Will Ferrell movie and to have a sleepover but didn't bother to invite Kenneth. "They talk trash on the court when they don't think I'm listening, then they make plans to do things right in front of Kenneth, as if he is not," she thought to herself. Through it all Kenneth stayed silent.

I met Kenneth when he was in the middle of eighth grade. He was just thirteen at a point when many of his classmates were already turning fourteen. Even so, he was tall for his age, good-looking, naturally athletic, and was starting on high-level competitive athletic travel teams. He got straight As in school, played a musical instrument, and was never a behavior problem at home or school. Academics, athletics, and music all came easy for him.

Friendships with peers did not.

Kids liked him, but few of his classmates ever gave him the time of day outside of school. He'd come home after sports practice, do his homework, play video games, and spend a lot of time on Instagram, looking at everyone else's social life. His parents wanted me to help him with his self-confidence, damaged by years of being left out, and to help him learn how to connect.

Then there was Nick.

I met Nick when he was fifteen and in his freshman year of high school. Similar to Kenneth, Nick was very bright academically, got very good grades in school (he eventually went on to get admitted to every college he applied to, including some of the most prominent ones in the country). Nick was clean-cut, good-looking, an athlete who played on two teams, and also very kind. He was intellectually curious, read numerous news sites, and was more current about world events than many adults I meet, myself included.

Kids liked him enough in school, but no one invited him to do anything outside of it. His efforts to make plans on weekends often were met with comments like "Yeah, let me see what I'm doing this weekend and get back to you," which Nick learned meant no. Nine times out of ten, they wouldn't even get back to him. He was convinced he had the least-texted phone in his high school. By the time I met Nick, he was spending countless hours on the Internet, descending deep into a world of social isolation, starving for social stimulation.

As is the case with many young teens like Nick and Kenneth, adults really liked them. "He connects really easily with people who are older than him, and little kids love him," I frequently hear about teens like them. "All our friends describe how mature he is and are impressed by how he can hold a mature conversation with them. But then we have get-togethers with other families, and all the other boys and girls his age are off together, and he sits awkwardly on the outside. It's painful to watch as a parent."

The big difference between Kenneth and Nick is that Kenneth was a moderate introvert (somewhere just below the midpoint line), and Nick was a high extrovert. Kenneth would have been more than happy just to have a few friends to hang out with, and because he got some of this in school and through sports, it wasn't nearly as hard for him to have his social life be this way as it was for his parents to witness it.

Nick, on the other hand, was really struggling, so starved for social contact that sometimes he would overwhelm people with his pent-up energy, which could turn them off. For example, it was almost impossible for him not to get into a debate about things, simply because he was starved for the stimulation. I distinctly remember cautioning his parents about how they needed to be prepared because when the work I was going to do with him kicked in, and Nick put the pieces in place, he was "going to do a lot of making up for lost time." And, boy, did he ever.

Then there is Jenny. Jenny had a great group of friends who slept over at each other's houses on weekends, played together every day, and included each other in everything. Then came seventh grade, when two of the girls branched out and started doing things on their own. First it was the time they went to the county fair without Jenny. Then it was the way they started "going shopping" without her, as more and more they cared about how they looked, what brands they wore, and the status they conferred. Jenny missed the days when the girls would be content baking cookies late at night, having spontaneous dance parties in her basement, and playing silly games in the backseat of the car on long rides.

Now her friends were busy Instagramming, gossiping about other girls, trying to impress boys, and, more and more, not eating cookies because "they go straight to your hips." Each new rejection or snarky comment from these girls made Jenny feel like a social outcast—weird, childish, and stupid.

Jenny didn't know whether there was something wrong with her that she was just not into this stuff, especially since every teen show on TV seemed to present it all as what teen girls are supposed to do. But Jenny couldn't make herself care about that. To her, eighth-grade boys were not interesting or fun enough to invest her time in. The desire to connect romantically or sexually had not awoken in her yet. She wasn't done with the innocent fun of childhood and couldn't understand why her friends had moved on.

Often, parents of young teens like Jenny don't know what to believe, either. Should their teen leave behind some of these "childlike" things and start to behave more age-typically for the times? Should their daughter start to dress differently now and take an interest in fashion? Should their son stop reading so much Harry Potter and get into what's "cool" with teens his age? The answer is no and yes and yes and no—in other words, learning to understand what is going on, developing the skills needed to navigate it, and building social competency is essential. The question isn't "if," it is "when" and "just how much?"

These young teens do need to start learning about the changing landscape of peer culture that happens during these years. Social puberty is going on in their world, even if they themselves have not yet gone through their own social puberty. But there is no need to rush into anything.

The culture we live in often forces youth into situations they have neither the sophistication nor the readiness to manage. It happens in schools with the work demands. It happens outside of schools with the social demands. Last summer I sat at a local community pool where a local day camp had hired a DJ to play music while the campers swam that afternoon. My seven-year-old was busy playing in the pool and our one-and-a-half-year-old was asleep on my shoulder as I sat on a chair in the shade. Then, the DJ started spinning his "booty" collection: Meghan Trainor's "All About That Bass," Sir Mix-a-Lot's "I Like Big Butts." I watched as many of the day camper kids jumped out of the water, shouted the lyrics out, and shook their butts around as they danced on the side of the pool. Many of them were barely eight or nine years old.

I was outraged. I would have been over-the-top outraged if my kids had been signed up for that camp and I'd found that the camp was exposing my children to that kind of message without my consent.

After my little one woke up, I pulled aside the manager of the pool, who concurred with my opinion that the music was really inappropriate for the age: "A number of the lifeguards agree—they're college students who think it is absurd for young kids to be hearing this." The generation gap thing is already happening, even at their age! What was most absurd to me wasn't that the incident happened but how many of these young kids seemed to already know all the words to these songs along with the dance moves. My children didn't and still don't. Some day they will, whether because we introduce it to them, access to media does, or the culture of their peers does, but that doesn't mean they will sing them or dance them or that they will ever have to.

> The generation gap thing is already happening, even at their age!

This is something I find many modern parents seem to have forgotten. There is no law that dictates that you must give your kids electronic devices, access to media, expensive clothes, money to eat out all the time, and so on. If CPS can't take your kids away from you for doing it or not, you have freedom to decide what is the best way to raise them. At what age should your teen have things like a cell phone, social media accounts, unrestricted access to the Internet, or a TV or computer in their room? My answer is always the same: It depends on two things—your values and who your child is.

The bigger issue is to realize that they must become equipped to live in a world where these things exist. They must learn to be able to navigate their way through them and around them. They must develop a capacity to manage them and use them, otherwise they wind up being used and managed by them.

With Kenneth, much of the work I did was to help him develop more social adeptness in how he communicates with his peers, but the bigger piece was teaching him how to find the right peers to be spending his time with. This is always the critical piece. This meant to stop looking at Instagram images of all the "popular" kids and instead start making plans with the ones who were more like him— the ones who also didn't drink and didn't smoke weed, the ones who treated girls with respect, the ones who wanted to improve their basketball game rather than their "game" with girls.

As an athlete, Kenneth was exposed to a lot of "locker room" humor and boy trash talk. There were constant comments and insults going around, bashing everyone from gays to girls to anyone who was the least bit different. Kenneth got more than his share of comments from the boys on his teams as they took their shots at him, claiming it was all in good humor. As he went into high school, more and more of them started drinking, smoking weed, and hooking up with multiple girls in a night. They bragged about it, made jokes about it, and essentially promoted every value Kenneth's parents despised. While Kenneth thought all of it was just stupid, he was also bothered by it. Too many times they made comments that got a laugh at his expense, and at times it pushed him to the point of rage. But he wasn't good at making "comebacks," and throwing out insults did not come naturally to him. He opted instead to just swallow it, go home, and distract himself with video games.

I continually pointed out to him that for every ten boys who acted that way, there were always a few others who did not. He needed to recognize this and consider reaching out to those boys. Eventually, he started to, and some friendships began to emerge. I also worked with his parents to help them to accept who their son is: he's not a high extrovert, and it really is okay that he doesn't do a ton of socializing. It's hard to be a boy like him in a culture that pushes so many boys to be sarcastic, sexist, and stupid. I remember one particular moment where a light bulb went on for his mom. It came after a long, involved series of interactions with other parents and their sons, and she had a moment similar to the one Lindsey's mom had where she really "got" the world her teens are living in and the pressures they feel as parents, too: She wrote in a text to me, "It's becoming so much clearer to me what the real work is here ... helping him coexist in this Neanderthal boy culture while encouraging his social ties with kids more like him values wise... I'm learning!"

With girls like Jenny, the work is to slowly introduce her to the reasons her friends are changing, doing it with a mix of playfulness about how "silly" some of their motivations are, coupled with a very serious message about how this is not going to go away and is only going to get more complicated. I give girls like her very practical "how-to" advice when she asks how to handle things or what to say to someone. I keep it simple and, at the same time, keep reassuring her of her own worth.

With Nick, the work was to teach him a ton of social and interpersonal communication skills. He truly needed to learn how to enter into conversations without overtaking them, how to read cues, how to flirt.

And with all of these teens, everyone from Leah to Christopher, Kenneth to Nick, Lindsey to Jenny, to conversations I already have with my own children, the critical piece they need to learn is to *find the right people* to be friends with and to associate with. The right people may not be the popular ones, or they may be. They may not be the same people they grew up being best friends with, or they may be. What they will most definitely be are people whom they feel fully comfortable being with, whom they can trust and rely on and who share their values and interests.

"Far more important than having someone to go to the party with," I often say, "is having someone who will leave with you when it just isn't the right place for you to be."

The value of providing this kind of guidance, education, and support at this stage is that it typically yields enormous benefits and often very quickly. The more socially competent and capable they feel, the more confident they become. The more confident they become, the more secure they are. The more secure they are, the more stable they become. This stability leads to more emotional maturity, less mood swings, and a far greater capacity to keep perspective and stay calm and centered, regardless of what is going on around them.

Teens who master this stage of development are typically worlds beyond the masses who continue to struggle with social insecurity, often well into their adult lives.

Rather than be lost in "Will people like me?" they begin asking instead "Will I like these people?" Rather than worrying about what others are thinking, they begin to decide for themselves what really matters. Rather than engage in every conflict, they pick and choose which relationships matter enough to work through and which ones aren't worth the effort. When it clicks, it is palpably evident to anyone close to them.

When things clicked for Nick, his social life opened up. He began going to all sorts of get-togethers, from loud parties to small "kick backs," to camping with his newfound best buddies. One comment he made to me once was quite astute: "You know what I've realized, Jeff? Parties are a great place to meet people but a lousy place to get to know them."

> "Far more important than having someone to go to the party with," I often say, "is having someone who will leave with you when it just isn't the right place for you to be."

That's mastering social puberty. That's what happens when a teen realizes he is "cool enough"— when he realizes that while there will always be more to learn about relationships and how to manage them, he can learn it.

It's at that point that the next stage of development has already begun to kick in.

chapter
seven

Crossing the Second Bridge:
The Great Awakening
"Who Am I, and Where Am I Going?"

This text message from Tanner came in at 11:03 p.m.:

"Jeff i need change. I dont think ive been myself for the past couple of years. And feel like i have a lot of learning and growth to do. i knew who i was before but now im in need of change and soul searching and tackling lots of issues. I dont know when i stopped being me. Can u help me figure this out? Not tonight but over the coming weeks?"

Tanner is seventeen years old. He has a life many other teens would envy. He's tall, good-looking, charming, extroverted, outgoing, athletic, and creatively talented (he plays the guitar and gets lead roles in his school's theater program). He also surfs and is equally as comfortable hanging out with the guys as he is with the girls. He has two best friends who are as cool, easygoing, and interesting as he is. Since he hit puberty there has been no shortage of girls, girls, and more girls in his life. This last year, he finally had his first serious girlfriend, too—a relationship with a brilliant, beautiful, soulful girl that lasted almost nine months.

His family has financial means and many connections. They take really cool vacations, and he has been to a lot of places and met really interesting people. His family can afford to send him to an exclusive private school and to make any college in the country available to him. Though he was diagnosed with ADD, between medication, tutors, family support, and, more than anything else, just plain hard work, he is getting almost straight As. At surface level, the world is his oyster. So why is he sending me such an ominous message so late on a school night? Is it just a moment where he lost his way? Is it just hormones distorting his thinking? Is he depressed?

Or is there something else going on?

If I were to handle this kind of thing in the conventional way, I'd either downplay it, saying he's had a rough day, or I'd rush to get him diagnosed with depression or generalized anxiety disorder and suggest weekly therapy sessions coupled with some kind of medication. The number of teens in communities like his who are in treatment just like that is astounding.

But I don't approach this kind of message in either of those ways; I don't downplay it, and I don't pathologize it. I read it as a sign that he is deeply entrenched in the second stage of development into becoming a young adult, the stage of needing to figure out who he is.

If the first stage is about social puberty and answering the questions "Am I cool enough?" and "Where do I fit in with my peers?" then the second stage becomes about answering the questions "Who am I?" and "Where do I fit in in the larger world?" These are much bigger questions to answer in complexity, scope, and consequences of the decisions. Answering them is also a journey.

This stage begins to happen in every healthy teen sometime between fifteen and a half and seventeen years old.

It is when teens have the realization that they are their own person, but they have little to no idea who that is. They realize that they have been who they needed to be, to be accepted by the peer groups, teams, or colleges they've wanted to be accepted by. They've been who their parents told them to be. Now they need to figure out who they are, independent of outside opinion and influence. For many teens, this is the stage of the greatest angst. How are they to make the right decisions for themselves?

Answering these questions happens through multiple ways: There are awakenings they have about life's truths and realizations they have about themselves. There are decisions they make about what values they want to live by and which ones they will discard. Lastly, there are threshold experiences they must have to fully integrate into themselves—the kinds of experiences where there is "the who I was before" and "who I am now and how I will subsequently live my life after."

> It is when teens have the realization that they are their own person, but they have little to no idea who that is.

97

The Awakenings

Contributing to both the complexity of answering these questions and the urgency that older teens feel to find the answers are a series of factors, mostly brought on by finally being old enough to see life in a more "real" and complex way. While there is no guarantee of the sequences of these realizations, they always include these:

- The realization that their parents (and all the adults in their lives) are not perfect, do not have all the answers, and cannot always protect them.

- The realization that their parents are not going to live forever, and therefore one day they will be on their own and must be able to make it without Mom and Dad.

- The realization that people their own age die and thus that they too are mortal.

- The realization that in spite of their fantasies and the well-intentioned pep talks from caregivers and motivational speakers, they are not going to be able to do anything they want with their lives. (I distinctly remember the day when I was sixteen years old, and I realized I was done growing. I would never be taller than average and would never dunk a basketball, and my dreams of playing in the NBA were over.)

- The realization that corruption exists, is rampant, and will likely always exist. Whether it takes the form of racism, sexism, anti-Semitism, political corruption, favoritism, or star athletes going down for steroid use, this awakening is unavoidable.

I remember one of the most profound moments of awakening in my own life happening when I was sixteen. My parents offered me their tickets to attend a performance of a professional traveling Broadway theater group who were doing a show at the Civic Center Theatre in my hometown of Peoria, Illinois. Peoria was a very blue-collar town, with a white-collar element that fed off the unions who dominated the labor force. If it weren't for being the world headquarters for Caterpillar Tractor Company and home to Bradley University, Peoria would best be known for being the hometown of Richard Pryor (who was raised in a brothel) and where old-school vaudeville acts in the 1920s and 1930s either launched into legitimacy or went to die. Well, playing in Peoria this night was a musical tribute to the big band music of Duke Ellington, *Sophisticated Ladies*. It featured an all-black cast, with amazing dancing, brilliant horn sections, and an inspiring, up-tempo sequence of music and dancing.

When the show ended, my best friend John and I jumped to our feet and gave the cast an enthusiastic standing ovation. After a few seconds, John elbowed me and said, "Jeff, look around. We are the only ones standing!" I looked around, and it was true: 1,500 people in the auditorium and only two of us standing.

The next morning my father asked me about the show. I told him about the music and the dancing and choreography. Then I told him about the end and how odd it was that John and I were the only ones giving a standing ovation.

My father looked at me, then looked away with this distant glare … to a place that he would only go when there was something weighing on him. He turned back to me and in a somber tone said words which still echo with me today, "Well, son, it's time that you realize that you are growing up in a town where the only place a black man gets a standing ovation is on the basketball court."

I was sixteen and yet suddenly so much older. The illusion I held that I was living in this wholesome, kind Midwestern town gave way to the reality that there were gaping inequalities and issues here. It was the ultra-conservative, narrow, small-minded Midwest, even while it did still have a lot of really kind people … yes, including the kind of people who were only kind to their kind. I knew that day that there would come a time sooner than later that I would leave that town and not come back—that my place in the world was somewhere else.

A piece of my childhood died that day. But an even bigger piece of my adulthood, and learning who I really was and wanted to be, was born.

That's how it is when teens have these awakenings and can make it across the threshold. They feel like they have given up something and instantly gained something greater. When they don't get across that threshold, they get stuck. They get angry at the world for not being different and then become scared or insecure. They get stuck being an adolescent in a world that needs adults.

If this awakening and seeking hasn't begun by the time they turn eighteen, I grow concerned either that something is way off developmentally or that there may be some kind of undiagnosed organic issue happening. Rarely does anyone go through it any younger. I believe this is due to biology: brain development doesn't permit it.

What This Stage Can Look
Like from the Outside

Phone calls from concerned parents of teens this age are so common in my practice that I have even toyed with writing a book and just calling it *Sixteen*. The calls almost always begin the same: "My son or daughter is sixteen ..." Then they go on to describe significant changes in behavior—withdrawing from parents and/or friends, shifting friend groups, motivation issues with school, or questioning the meaning and purpose of all the things they must contend with, especially school. Sometimes I hear the stories about how parents discovered marijuana in the teen's closet and learned their teen is using it to go to sleep at night, claiming it is the only thing that helps them quiet their mind. The practice of self-medicating has begun. Sometimes they tell me that their teen is sleeping around with lots of partners, cheating in school or skipping it all together, buying Adderall to help them study for a test, dropping out of sports or activities they used to love, or talking about gap years or even not going to college, when they've never even considered that option before.

> "She's just not herself anymore." ... "It's like he's suddenly become this raging asshole who is angry at everyone" ... "We are worried she may be depressed." ... "He wants a medical marijuana card to get prescription THC to help him sleep at night." ... "He came and sat on my bed last night and described how something seems to be missing." ... "WHAT IS HAPPENING TO MY KID?"

They tell me stories about insomnia, panic attacks, and severe anxiety. Often their older teens are worried about their future, feeling like they are in a constant competition they're doomed to lose. No matter how well they do in school, there is someone doing better. No matter how many extracurricular activities they do, fifty of their classmates are doing more, and they fear that colleges will find them more interesting and appealing. It is no wonder that so many teens this age wind up in clinical treatment of one form or another.

The problem as I see it is that the issue causing them to feel so out of balance, worried, and unstable is not resolvable by treating it like an illness, because it isn't one. It is the by-product of being in the midst of The Great Awakening into adulthood—hearing the invitation to discover themselves, yet lacking the guidance, perspective, opportunities, or tools to manage the uncertainty and the intensity.

Let me share some stories about what does work.

chapter eight

Awakenings, Self-Realizations, Threshold Experiences, and Decisions

Answering the questions "Who am I, where am I going, where do I fit in in the world?" happens through multiple ways.

Awakenings

Eighteen-year-old Mateo plopped himself down on a reclining chair in my office one afternoon a few years ago. I used to refer to him as "Pretty Boy" because he dressed so preppy, never had a hair out of place and had that Justin Bieber-like boyish charm that the girls seemed to love. Like many of the teens I work with, he was bright, thoughtful, sincere, and going places with his life.

It was the spring of his senior year of high school, and he had already been admitted to a prestigious university, where he was enrolled to start the next fall. He was a month or two away from graduating from an exclusive private high school, one that prided itself on the high quality of its education and the comprehensive worldview and critical thinking skills it taught.

Mateo explained to me how they'd had yet another distinguished guest speaker come in to address the student body that day, delivering another message about the state of the world. His school prided itself on the caliber of speakers they brought in and the range of topics their expertise covered. He'd heard from leading research scientists, pioneers in green technology, members of Congress, CEOs of major international businesses, and Laureate writers.

"You know what I realized today, Jeff?" he asked me. "In four years at my school, there was only one speaker who was a conservative or Republican—just one! And he was on a panel with a bunch of Democrats and was booed by the students almost every time he spoke. My school has basically brainwashed all of us to think like liberals and to treat anyone who isn't a Democrat like they are idiots."

That line "Do you know what I realized today?" is one of the cues I listen for that tells me a teen is in this stage.

"What do you think about that?" I then asked.

"I think it's hypocritical. They say they are teaching us to think globally, but really they are just teaching us to think the way they want us to. It makes me wonder how many other things I've been taught to believe that I may not agree with if I knew the other side."

We spoke for most of the next few hours about many things; realizing the power the adults in his world have had to expand or limit his thinking, the challenging task it is to truly be a critical thinker and particularly the task to seek truth rather than to just try to prove oneself right. It was a very adult conversation. By the time it was over, he was one big step forward on his journey to adulthood, and the momentum that was in place would only further him in this direction.

Michelle's Dad

Michelle, seventeen, recently called me up and said, "I realized this weekend that my dad is actually a really good guy. For years I have heard my mom talk about what an asshole he is, but the truth is, he's a really good guy."

I've had many such conversations with teens who grew up in divorced homes listening to one spouse trash-talk the other. Certainly there are times the criticism is warranted, but more often than not the teen awakens to the truth. Sometimes, it goes the other way, like the time sixteen-year-old Jared came in and told me about how he had accidently broken a video game he'd purchased at Best Buy. His mom, who happens to be lawyer, took him back to get a new one, and as they were walking in the door she turned to him and said, "Let me do the talking." She then proceeded to lie to the store manager, claiming it was broken when they bought it. Her lie worked. He replaced it at no charge.

Jared told me the story, and I asked, "So why are you telling me this?"

"Because I want to know what you think."

"I think you already know what I think," I said. "The more important question is, what do you think?"

Conversations like this are not always pleasant or comfortable. These are sometimes agonizing moments of awakening for a teen, especially when it comes to seeing their parents' flaws and coming to terms with their parents' fallibility. Guiding them through this means getting them beyond their emotional reaction to it, to accepting life as it is, and then, most importantly, deciding for themselves who they want to be and how they want to behave in the world in spite of what others do, or, in some cases, because of what others do.

Self-Realizations

Remember Lindsey from the party that got out of hand when she was a freshman in high school? This story happened four years later, midway through her freshman year at the University of Southern California.

It was the end of her winter break, and as we often do when she is in town, we met at one of her favorite sushi restaurants. Lindsey had been grappling with feeling out of sorts, a feeling that had been growing as her first semester at USC unfolded. She was questioning if maybe she'd made the wrong choice, was considering transferring, and was not sure what to do. She'd joined a "popular" sorority where she had made many social connections and was doing lots of partying. She was doing well academically, though her freshman year classes were less than inspiring. As she told me about her life, it became evident to me what was missing. Now it was time to make it evident to her.

During her high school years, in addition to being popular and having a huge social life, she'd also gotten involved with her school's mock trial team. By her senior year of high school, she was not only one of the leaders of the team that had competed at the state finals four years in a row, she was also voted one of the best in the state of California. This experience had inspired her. She had decided that she wanted to go into law and was determined to be the kind of lawyer who contributed to helping those in need, not the kind who just helped make money for people who already have money. She was interested in women's issues, minority rights issues, and environmental issues. But attending law school and becoming a lawyer were a long way from being a popular sorority girl taking undergraduate freshman Gen Ed survey courses.

As the sushi arrived at the table, it was finally my turn to speak. "Has it occurred to you that maybe you are not at the wrong school but you are just consumed with winning at the wrong game?"

"What do you mean?"

"You're getting caught up at winning the social climbing game with a bunch of ditzy sorority girls. It's like you want to be queen of the ditzes! It may not say much about your worth to the world, but at least as you walk around campus you have bragging rights that you excel at dumbing yourself down to whatever level it takes to be at the top of that scene. It's too bad you are not blond. It would just be too cliché ..." I am not afraid to speak so bluntly and critically to my clients. I do it because, for a personality like Lindsey has, it works. I also do it because I build enough credibility with them that they allow me to. They also know that I can be equally as complimentary if that is what will help them get what they want.

"That's harsh … and I don't think you understand …" Lindsey responded quickly.

"No, I don't think you understand!" I interrupted. "You're not just smart, you're competitive—*really* competitive. And you have a part of you that cares deeply about the world and the way you use your talents to impact it. Don't just ignore that and put it off until you graduate. If you are going to compete and win at something, why not make it something that, when you win at it, will actually matter to you and make you feel good?"

"Like what?" she asked.

"You loved mock trial when you were in high school. You rocked when you were in intense debates. You're considering law school; why don't you get a job or internship doing something on behalf of the legal rights of disenfranchised people or a cause that you care about? Why not start being too busy for the social climbing BS and start spending time learning something and helping people who could use your help?"

"Like what? They only give law internships to law school students!"

"And you are going to let something as stupid as a stupid policy stop you? C'mon, where is the competitive side of you? When they say, "Sorry you aren't old enough," convince them that they need you. Be the first freshman in the history of USC to do a graduate level internship… start there!"

"Where would I go?" she asked with growing enthusiasm.

"I'd start with organizations that advocate for people you are concerned about. You tell me! It takes 60 seconds to Google it and see what organizations are out there. Imagine what it would be like to spend your Thursday sitting in court next to a high-profile attorney, helping her defend someone who is being taken advantage of by a corrupt system. Contrast that with spending the same Thursday worrying about which pair of Jimmy Choo's you should wear to be popular that day."

"Very good one, Jeffrey ... surprised you know about Jimmy Choo's!"

"Hey, whenever I buy $2,000 shoes for my wife, I always but Jimmy Choo's!"

"In other words, never?"

"Damn right! I am too busy doing things I care about to go shopping for shoes!"

After lunch, we parted ways and agreed to talk again in a few weeks—as we have for years. I sent her links to some organizations that would be right up her alley. The rest was up to her.

Two weeks to the day after her return to school, I got this text: "Hey Jeff, I got an internship at the district attorney's office!"

When we spoke later that day, she filled me in on what it took to get an internship with the district attorney's office. As expected, when she initially inquired, she learned that they only offer internships to law students. By the time she was done working her magic, she had not only secured an interview with them but with one of the leaders of the department. She was offered an internship on the spot. Not only was she the first freshman from her school to secure such an internship, she was also the first for the DA's office.

Since that day, she is "herself" again. Sorority life is just one part of her life now, rather than an all-consuming identity. She appreciates that it offers lots of socializing for when she wants a break from the work and demands of school. At this writing, she's spending the summer in an internship at ACLU headquarters in Washington, D.C. She is growing more and more clear about who she is, what she wants, and where she is headed. That's what someone her age should be doing, so that's what I do with people in her stage of development. It is interesting how returning to the right path in life not only makes her excited about life again but also makes her both attracted to and attractive to a different type of person or opportunity.

The Girl Who Came in Second

Sometimes the realization a teen needs to have is not so obvious: Anna's parents owned and ran a local shop working side by side and modeling a really healthy marriage. As Anna was their only child and was born a little bit later in their lives, she was definitely the apple of her parents' eyes. Her dad heard me speak at Anna's high school one night toward the end of her tenth-grade year. He contacted me the next day to discuss some concerns he had about Anna. He explained how while their soon-to-be sixteen-year-old daughter had great grades in school, she seemed to be constantly struggling with self-confidence and with friends who were unreliable. Like so many parents I talk to, they couldn't quite put their finger on what exactly it was, but they really knew she needed something to help her see in herself all the positive traits that were evident to so many others.

Anna walked through the door to my office a few days later and made an immediate impression on me. She had a stunning smile, bright red flowing hair, and a genuine sweetness about her that made her instantly likeable. At the surface level, it's hard to fathom how someone like her could have trouble socially. She is charming, funny, attractive, and, while she was no serious athlete, joined a few teams just to stay in shape and connect with others. She had friends, but they were unreliable. Too often they'd cancel plans at the last minute, occasionally just blatantly lying to her about why. She'd begun to grow mistrusting of others and, worse, doubted herself, questioning if there was something unattractive or off-putting about her. Why wouldn't they always just invite her, too?

I quickly realized that Anna was like those girls who look in the mirror and see someone very different than the rest of the world does, someone far less attractive or appealing than they actually are. Her challenge was that she lacked any real perspective to assess who she is. She thought "way too small" of herself. At sixteen, it was time to begin figuring this out. But the journey to that realization is rarely brief or direct. Anna was just beginning this journey. I needed to get her caught up quickly.

> Like so many parents I talk to, they couldn't quite put their finger on what exactly it was, but they really knew she needed something to help her see in herself all the positive traits that were evident to so many others..

I spent much of that year getting to know her, giving her social puberty advice that I give to someone who is in Stage 1 (because many teens still need this). I also subtly began shifting her thinking about her social world and herself, giving her fresh perspective: "You know that girl Carly you hang out with is really incredibly self-absorbed and not trustworthy," or "The way that Tommy ditched his friends at the party to leave with that girl was really shitty behavior. How did he think they were going to get home? Oh yeah, he didn't think about it. He wasn't thinking with that head. You've got to watch out for guys like that."

As her year went on, Anna became more socially sophisticated and began to take things less personally, but she still kept hanging out with kids who were too self-absorbed to offer her the kind of relationships she wanted. My work was knowing when was the right moment to confront her with it in a way that was more than just commonsense advice—because threshold moments rarely happen with commonsense advice.

The moment finally arrived when she wrote a personal essay for school that got very graphic and deep about her feelings. Her teacher read it, panicked, and called the school counselor, who called her parents. They were concerned she might be depressed, or worse, suicidal. Apparently, she mentioned in the essay feeling depressed about how no guy ever asks her out and wondering what the point of it all was. It is understandable how this could be interpreted that way. I did not underestimate what it might mean, though I doubted it was as serious as it sounded.

I was speaking at a conference in Los Angeles the day this happened and immediately called her mom back when I got the message. I encouraged her parents to let her stay home from school the next day so that we could meet. I flew home late that night and met Anna at my office the next morning.

When she walked in she immediately told me how embarrassed she was and assured me many times over that she was not depressed or suicidal. She explained to me how frustrated she gets that even with all the new skills and confidence she has acquired, she continues to not get the guy. "Why am I always the one having to take the first step or make the first move? Why do the guys I like always wind up with some other girl? I'm almost seventeen years old, and I am starting to think I'm going to wind up being an old maid living with a hundred cats!"

It is typical at this age for teens to desire to have real intimacy, emotionally and physically. For those like Anna who were really ready, not having it can be agonizing and feels incredibly lonely. She then went on to vent her frustrations about her friends who were flaky and the classmates she was with in different class projects who were never as committed as she is, leaving most of the work to fall on her shoulders. Here she was sitting in front of me, raw with emotion and as transparent as she could be. I listened quietly for probably twenty minutes, simply nodding my head. Finally she stopped talking and the room got quiet ... awkwardly quiet. I just stared at her.

"Okay," she finally broke the silence. "Aren't you going to respond? Going to give me some of those Jeff pearls of wisdom? How about a pep talk like everyone else gives me—you know, the one that goes "Oh, Anna, you are so beautiful, and one day someone is going to see this and sweep you off your feet"?

"Actually," I said when I finally spoke, "I am just going to ask you one question." I paused, letting the silence stretch.

"And that is ...?" she finally demanded.

"At what point in your life did you decide that you were the girl who always comes in second place?" I asked bluntly. Then I just sat and stared at her. She stared back at me, not certain what to make of this.

After about thirty seconds of silence, she asked, "What do you mean?"

"Anna, you know exactly what I mean! You go into all these situations expecting to come out disappointed ... expecting to come in second place!" I repeated and then paused again while it sank in.

Then I continued, "I have known you for something like six months, and, yeah, I agree you are beautiful and smart and all that stuff, and yeah, most likely one day some man is going to see you and be ready for you but certainly not these little weenie boys you keep wasting your time with. And I think your pouting about the way people keep flaking on you and how your classmates are lazy and how the guys you want to be with always choose the other girl is just the rambling of a girl who has decided that she's the one who comes in number two. In fact, that's so much the way things are with you that you don't even realize that you are attracted to people who will take you for granted or how you send signals that it is okay to take you for granted, so even people who otherwise wouldn't treat you this way end up doing it because you teach them to. You let them all off the hook, not because you are okay with it but because you actually believe that you are the kind of person who just gets treated this way! So what am I supposed to say? 'Poor Anna, what a tragedy it is that no one sees her real beauty,' and then start singing my own rendition of 'Someday My Prince Will Come'? I mean, I will if you want me to..."

She just sat there listening, taking it in. A tear formed in her eye. When she finally spoke, all she could say was, "Wow. That's not what I was expecting to hear. It's not what I wanted to hear. But I have to confess, I think it is what I *needed* to hear."

"You *think*? Or you *know*?"

"I know!" she confessed. "On some level I think I have known this all along. I've been playing this role as the doormat and the responsible one and the one who is there for everyone else for so long, that I guess I forgot who I am."

"Forgot who you are?" I replied. "Or are just figuring out now that that is not who you are? That in fact who you are is a kick-ass, smart, talented, beautiful girl whose standards are too high to settle for lame creeps like that guy Tommy, but who is also someone who that really cool boy in your AP Chemistry class should get off his ass and ask to Homecoming?"

In subsequent conversations we spoke about when it is good to be number two and when it only gets in her way and needs to stop. As she was interested in film, I made it very clear that there is nothing wrong with being an assistant producer for a career, at least until she finally is ready to take the number one role.

Anna didn't get the date she wanted to Homecoming, but she went anyway. She confidently approached that boy from AP Chemistry, and by Christmas through the end of senior year they were dating. And he treated her well—really well. She stepped up and became a director in her Film and Media Production class, leading two all-school projects and receiving much acclaim. She went on to a highly regarded film school for college. While there was another period of adjustment in the new environment, and some of the old demons revisited her, by sophomore year she had hit her groove and was well on her way into her womanhood and her Hero's Journey.

Bearing Witness

Many times their self-realizations come on their own. I learn about them because they excitedly want to share the news, eager for someone to bear witness to their evolution on their life journey. "I realized something about myself the other day ..." they typically begin. Then they go on with things like these I heard: "I'm really not a city person ... I like the outdoors and really need to be near it," "I was going to apply to a bunch of small colleges that my college counselor suggested, but now I realize I really want to be at a big school," or "I used to think I would definitely go to school and study business, but I actually really am interested in becoming a physical therapist. The human body just fascinates me."

This text message came in at 10:06 a.m. on a school day from sixteen-year-old Isabelle: "I just realized something. I realized that every girl has insecurities that lead them to act the way they do. The root of everything is not being good enough." She sent this from school, moments after the realization happened. She needed to share it with someone, not so that I would respond to it but so that it would be witnessed. No surprise, the conversation we did have several days later was rich with insights, and she was ripe for learning.

Seventeen-year-old Cassidy told me last week: "You know what I realized this weekend? I really can't stand most of the people I hang out with. I think I need a whole new group of friends. I really don't fit in with them. I hate the stupid things they do. I'm not one of them. "

Realizing this is big. Taking action to truly change this is even bigger. That's why I will likely have to push Cassidy over this threshold to actually change her friend group, leave behind the familiar, and step fully onto her journey to adulthood.

It is also at this stage that most teens who have sexual orientation or sexual identify differences "come out." The loneliness and pain of the dissonance they experience of hiding this truth about themselves comes at too high of a cost.

Womanhood, Not Girlhood

Gabrielle approached me as I was heading to my car to drive back to the airport. I'd been speaking to staff members and running training at the all-girls summer camp she worked at in the Northeast. Having worked with well over three hundred summer camps in the last twenty years, I'd had the privilege of meeting and interacting with thousands of college-aged teens and young adults from around the world. While the camp directors hire me to come in and teach skills about working with kids and to inspire their staff to take their roles in the lives of their campers as seriously as the director does, I've had countless side conversations with these staff members that were about personal issues in their lives. They almost always begin the same: "Can I ask you a question that isn't really about camp?" one of them says, waiting patiently to be the last one in line to speak with me after a formal training session.

Gabrielle's question was about a guy she was having an on-again off-again thing with while at camp. The details of their relationship are not important, but this chat on the steps outside their office, the beginning of my yearlong relationship of mentoring her, is. She was twenty-one years old and going into her senior year at a major university in the Washington, D.C. area. From the suburbs of Boston, she was the youngest of three kids and was convinced her parents would support this if she insisted it would have value to her.

I gave her my card and true to her word, her parents contacted me the next day. They expressed their perspective on her and their desire to have me help her "develop confidence and find direction." While her dad did most of the talking, her mom chimed in enough for me to know that Gabrielle was both a daddy's girl and her mom's youngest, who she still felt intensely protective of. We made an arrangement to work together, with my insistence that the rest needed to be between Gabrielle and me. She was twenty-one and less than a year from graduating from college. She needed to step up and make this her relationship, her agenda, and her work to be done.

Gabrielle and I spoke almost every week for the next year, sometimes multiple times in a week if a lot was going on. Though I live in California, I met with her in person several times that year, as I maintain an office on the East Coast and go there every six weeks or so.

Our conversations were often about the guy from camp (who lived far away the rest of the year, which made things more complicated) but regularly ventured into her social life on campus, the tutoring jobs she had picked up by word-of-mouth referral, and her fears and concerns with what she would do after graduation.

The one theme I was relentless about with her was the way in which she continually referred to herself as a "kid." At first I was nice about it. Then I annoyed her by constantly interrupting her when she would say it to correct her: "Say 'adult' or 'woman.'"

I would explain, "Gabrielle, you say you want me to help you be more confident and to figure out what you want for your future, but until you start thinking of yourself as an adult instead of just trying to *think like* one, you are just wasting your time. You have to stop being Mommy and Daddy's little girl. Stop approaching your relationships like a teen girl, and start approaching them like an adult woman *because you are one!*" When she pushed back, I would present the overwhelming evidence about her adulthood being so obvious. They'd typically sound like this: "The reason these people keep hiring you to tutor and nanny their kids is because you are an *adult* whom they trust. I would hire you to take care of my own kids, and I know my wife would agree. When I hear about a teenager who babysits, I think, 'No, thanks,' because I can see them with the phone out, texting while my kid is falling out of a tree. With you, I can see you teaching my kids how to climb a tree safely. *You are not a kid. You are not a girl. You are an adult woman!"*

By March of that year, the message finally sank in. She stopped calling herself a "kid." She began sounding more confident. She became more decisive. She let the relationship with the guy come to an end, recognizing it was mostly just the fantasy of a girl, not based on the sound reasoning of an adult woman. Then she began thinking about getting a job in Australia, leaving the United States behind for the first time in her life. She'd grown up on the East Coast. She'd gone to camp on the East Coast. She went to college on the East Coast. She's basically spent her entire life never being more than a few hours drive from her parents.

Now she was ready to move to Australia ... and she did, spending a year there, working full time, building community, being independent. Not long after she came back, she was offered a leadership high-level responsibility job at a summer camp ... a job that they give to an adult.

Mentoring and Threshold Moments

During one of my HeroPath® programs in New Zealand a few years ago, I met Hayden. He was nineteen years old and just starting his second semester at University in Auckland. He was one of the leaders of the youth search and rescue organization that brought me over to run this program for the teens. Among his peers, Hayden was looked up to; he was knowledgeable, skilled, and had a commanding presence.

When he approached me at lunch the last day and asked if we could talk, I had no idea what it would be about. After we ate, we took a walk around the campus of the venue they'd rented for the program. He opened up to me about lacking confidence with girls. He told me about how there was this girl he really liked and who was clearly flirting with him and sending signals, but he couldn't bring himself to ask her out. He wanted my help getting more confidence. At nineteen and with so much else going for him, it was easy to wonder what had gone awry that he couldn't bring himself to ask out someone who was making it so easy. "She's out of my league," he explained.

That's when I understood. And I knew what needed to happen. So long as he thought of himself as belonging in a different league, he'd continue getting the same results. "People don't get what they want," my mentor and teacher Joseph Riggio had taught me. "They get what they *expect*."

I needed to change his expectations.

I recognized in that moment that Hayden was at the "threshold of adventure," as Joseph Campbell would call it. His desire to have the experience was immense. His readiness to do what it took was prime. All he needed was someone he trusted and respected to do what I did with him in the twelve minutes we spent walking around the field that afternoon.

This is the role of the mentor—to help get the hero across that initial threshold and launch fully into the journey of his life. At this stage, it is to help him grow into himself, to leave behind the scared insecure boy he was, and to embrace the strong, capable young man he is. After hearing him talk about his fears, I asked him, "So what's her name?"

He stammered a bit and then said, "Kara."

"Okay, I'll have this talk with you—but just so you know, it is going to lead to you asking her out in the next twenty-four hours if not sooner but certainly not later." Then before he could reply and leave open the possibility of not doing it, I said, "So tell me about Kara and why you are choosing her as the girl you are going to ask out later today. I need to know a little about her to make sure I give you good advice on how to ask a girl like her out." I made certain the conversation moved quickly, and when I'd heard enough, I immediately went into the kinds of things he could actually say to make it happen.

"But what if she says no?" he asked. Boys like him always ask this question.

"Then you'll know she is not available and you can still look yourself in the mirror tonight and be proud of yourself that you got over the hurdle and did it," I replied. "You win no matter what she says."

"This is so far out of my comfort zone!" he exclaimed.

"Singling one girl out of the 3.5 billion girls on earth should be." I answered. "That's what makes it so special." He liked that answer.

I looked at my watch. It was time to get back to the group. Only twelve minutes had passed, yet to him, a whole stage of his life had passed. It was as if it had already happened, just not yet. He was going to do this that night. His childhood practice of staying in the comfort zone and thinking of himself as an undesirable boy was over. He was already standing a bit taller.

That was around 2 p.m. Sunday. I got this email from him when my plane landed back in the United States, just thirty-six hours later: "Hey Jeff... I did it. I got her phone number, called her last night, and asked if she wanted to meet up. We met up today, and the first thing I asked her was if she wanted to go out on a date with me. *She instantly said yes!*"

Unlike a teen in the social puberty stage who needs to have skills and successes to know they are okay, a teen in this stage needs to know things about themselves before and without the external successes that substantiate it. That's what makes this about identity and sense of self. Hayden had become his own man the moment he knew he was a man who had a voice and could use it, even when circumstances weren't going to make it easy. His sense of himself both expanded and solidified in that moment.

With Hayden it took twelve minutes.

With Anna it took six months for the moment to be right.

With Gabrielle it took nine months of delivering the same message in a hundred different ways a thousand times.

But with Faheem it took one lunch and one very unusual suggestion.

Decisions
The Other Oxford

- -

I met Faheem at a program I ran in Oxford, UK. At age 15¾, he was the youngest student at one of the most elite schools in Europe. Students who attended this college (the equivalent of an elite prep school in the United States) went on to the most select universities in the world. As has become the method at top-performing preparatory schools, learning at this school was done through either one-to-one tutoring or in very small, customized groups. There were none of the large classroom distractions here.

The students came from all over Europe, Asia, Africa, and the Middle East, the sons and daughters of politicians, world-class investors, renowned specialists, and leaders of some very big businesses. Faheem was from the Middle East. His father owned oil companies, granting his son the kind of wealth and power that allowed him to live like royalty. His family was so powerful and connected that initially they'd wanted bodyguards to be with Faheem while he was in England. As it was, embassy employees came up from London to regularly check on him.

Faheem was at a demanding school and under the microscope of almost constant surveillance, with the expectation that he'd one day take over a billion-dollar business. To say he felt like he was in a constant pressure cooker was an understatement. He was not even sixteen, and his childhood was mostly gone.

Gone were the days of coming home from school, rushing through homework, and rushing off to play soccer with his friends. Gone were the sleepovers, sleeping in, and eating leftovers from the refrigerator late at night. He was in Oxford now. He had business to attend to, and the clock was ticking.

The HeroPath® program I ran that weekend was attended by twenty-four students. They ranged in age from Faheem at nearly sixteen to a twenty-year-old Russian boy whose father worked alongside the mayor of Moscow. To say the least, it was an interesting bunch.

We were only there because the founders of the school were among the most visionary, progressive educators I've ever met. They were committed to the growth and development of the whole person, not just their grades and exam scores. Like me, they recognized the profound importance of helping teens in Stage 2 of this journey, to figure out who they are and where they are going. And as some of the teens in this group were quite literally going to step into positions of great power and influence, anything that could be done to grow their humanity and compassion could truly change the world.

There were a lot of personalities in the room, some of them very big. Because they were older than Faheem and didn't have to deal with their embassy, they had more freedom to come and go from campus; they could go out to the pubs and have wild nights on the rare nights they weren't up late studying.

Most of the weekend, Faheem just sat in the room quietly, almost invisible. With all the big personalities, it was easy not to notice him. At lunch on Sunday, I saw him going off to sit by himself, so I pulled up a chair and sat down with him.

As Faheem and I spoke, I found him really easy to engage one on one. He was thoughtful, articulate, bright, and sincere. I quickly learned about his family background and of his genuine interest in science. As he explained more about the circumstances and all the supervision, it became immediately evident how much the pressure was taking a toll on him. "I can't even go out and play football," he explained. "The school doesn't have a team, and the local club team meets during hours when I am supposed to be either in a tutoring session or studying. If not that, then the place they meet is across town, and it is not okay for me to go there without an escort."

The more we spoke, the more I understood how frustrated he was, pent up physically and isolated socially. "I feel like I have forgotten how to talk to people," he explained. "I just get quiet when I am around others. No one really knows my real personality."

"But when you are back home, out on the pitch with your teammates, or hanging out with your friends, who are you?"

"I'm loud, funny, assertive ... you could say I was a leader."

"So, Faheem, since you are sitting here with me in my program, and this is my specialty, do you want my input?" I asked.

"Sure," he said. I could tell he was just grateful to have someone paying attention, someone to bear witness to his life.

"I think you need to *decide* who you are," I explained. "Are you this quiet, shy, pent-up kid who you've become since you've been in England, or are you the loud, funny, assertive leader you are back home? You have to choose. Who you are doesn't change just because of the country you happen to be in. You can't let outside circumstances impact you this much if you are truly a leader. This one is your decision—who do you want to be?"

Without hesitation, he sat up and said, "The person I am at home."

"Then here's what I want you to do," I began, "realizing that it's going to sound strange and be out of your comfort zone—but it is going to work."

He sat up in anticipation. "What is it?"

"I want you to go talk to a stranger. Literally, get up, walk out of here, go up to someone on the street or in a shop, and strike up a conversation."

"How am I supposed to do that? What am I supposed to say?"

"In my experience, most people like talking about themselves, so just go ask people about themselves!" I explained. We spent another 15 minutes talking about the subtle details of how to do this.

Then he went and did it. When the group reconvened after lunch, there was no Faheem to be found. Fortunately the embassy didn't show up at that moment. But a half-hour later when he returned, I can say that the real Faheem showed up.

He was standing taller, he was animated—a different person. The story about the Italian store owner down the street with whom he'd just had coffee and whose life story he'd heard was not only funny but was told in a very entertaining way. He had the group laughing. He was charismatic, poised, and confident. A few months later we emailed each other and he reported that he was doing great, had made lots of new friends, and even found a way to be playing soccer.

When I went back a year later, he had just been elected class president, a different person than the quiet boy who sat invisibly in the training room a year earlier. He was astute, confident, charismatic, the kind of young man who could grow up to be the CEO of a major international company ... and run it ethically. With the right guidance, he *decided* what kind of person he was going to be, and he crossed the threshold that must inevitably be crossed to get there.

Do I or Don't I: A Ninety-Second Conversation about Cocaine

Abby called me one night during her freshman year of college. Her friends were planning to do cocaine that night, and she needed to decide if she was going to try it too. She called to ask my opinion.

I replied, "Abby, at this point there are only two reasons you call me: (1) Because you are in a situation that is complicated and you want my perspective and opinion on how you can handle it, or (2) because you already know what the right answer is for yourself, and you just want me to affirm it. Which one is this?"

Her reply, "Thank you. That is all I needed to hear."

She never needed to make a call like that again. Too often these breakthrough opportunities are missed because the adults in their lives resort to sermons and lectures, when what is really needed is trust.

Not If But When

In the fall of her sophomore year of high school, sixteen-year-old Kelsey's best friend lost her virginity. She was only fifteen years old. As the year went on, more of Kelsey's classmates became sexually active. By spring, she began to feel like she was the last virgin left in America. When an upperclassman invited her to prom that spring, then proceeded to express interest in her beyond just a prom date, she had a decision to make. Her friend was encouraging her to "do it," even giving her advice on birth control. The older boy was overtly making opportunities available where they could be alone at his home.

Kelsey knew that he wasn't "boyfriend material," because he'd made it clear he wasn't looking for a serious, committed relationship. Even so, he was cute, more experienced than she, interested in her, and she had to decide.

My teen girl clients are incredibly candid with me about this topic. I've had this conversation with many of them over the years: How do you decide when is the right time and with who? For Kelsey, this was a critical Stage 2 moment: Who was she going to be? Just another typical teen girl who has sex on prom night? Or would she hold out and be the girl who waits for someone who truly cares about her, as she'd always thought she would do?

In today's teen social world, the pervasive cultural norm is to be casual about sex. The attitude many teens have is that waiting for real love is not only old-fashioned, it's probably a waste of time. This seems especially true because so many of today's boys with their porn-influenced attitudes lack the maturity to have a "real" relationship.

I told her that she would need to make her own decision about this, and what I could offer was to point out some things about herself that were important to consider when making this decision. One of them is that she is the kind of person who grows very attached to people very quickly. I reminded her that she has long been a "hopeless romantic" type, and the list of Hugh Grant-style romantic comedy movies she wanted me to watch when I first met her. In my experience, those are not things that change overnight. Ultimately she needed to just decide what kind of person she was going to be regarding this aspect of life. Once she decided, she could move forward, more sure of herself and more confident in her choices.

I often remind my clients that the easier choices are not always the best ones or the right ones. Making these life value decisions before they actually get into these situations makes it a lot easier to act on them when they finally are in them.

On a Different Path

At twenty years old and two years into college, Nico realized that he was in the wrong place, pursuing the wrong field. He tried to ignore it, but things only got worse: "I felt like a shell of myself, just going through the motions … It got to a point where I felt like my body was there but my mind was somewhere else." This could have been a reason to be diagnosed with a mental illness and to go on medication; instead it was the realization that led to a quantum breakthrough in his answering the question, "Who am I, and where am I going?"

This self-realization led to a very difficult, yearlong journey that led him to move back home and take prerequisite classes at a community college so that he could eventually transfer into an architecture school. During that year it was hard to watch his peers moving forward toward graduating college "on time." It was even harder to see all the Facebook and Instagram pictures of their "junior year abroad" experiences, while he was sitting on the couch in his mom's living room.

He's now enrolled in an architecture program at a different university, typically spending late nights in the studio, and while the work is hard and not always fun, he loves what he is learning and is excited about where it is heading. "Looking back on it now," he recently told a group of adults training to become coaches in my HeroPath® program, "I realize that so few of my old high school classmates are really excited about what they are going to do after college. I spent that year envying them and being embarrassed that I was so far behind, but now I feel like I'm actually really far ahead."

For Nico, leaving a four-year university to move home and attend community college was a life-changing threshold experience for him. It required courage to make that leap of faith, and he sought out a lot of help from me that year. "Jeff kept reminding me that this was only temporary and that I was being courageous to do it. I have to admit there were many times I didn't feel that way, but now I really get it. It has totally changed how I see myself now."

In my experience, there are many college students who are stuck where Nico was, studying the wrong thing, perhaps at the wrong place, and many will never take the bold step of doing something about it. The Threshold of Adventure, as Joseph Campbell called it, is a scary place, and many never get across it. Many never even try. I often tell me clients, "There's a reason it's called the Hero's Journey and not the Wimp's Journey! It takes courage to follow one's own unique path, especially when that means veering from the norms."

Hannah Found Her Voice, But It's Really a Story about Someone Else

When I met Hannah when she was sixteen, I immediately knew two things: this girl was going places with her life, and because of her sensitivity and deep morality, it wasn't going to be easy for her. I could write a book on the journey she's gone on to grow into the remarkable young woman she has become, professionally and personally.

Instead, I will only tell one story:

Hannah dated a string of guys through college, none of whom was ready to be serious. Often she was disappointed by the way they took her for granted or made excuses to not get serious. Like many young women, she too often allowed herself to not be treated well, out of fear of being seen as too needy, or worse, a bitch. "Oh, it's okay! I understand!" she would often say, when they would cancel plans on her last second. Inside though she was constantly berating herself for not being stronger. Building this kind of confidence and mind-set was the focus of much of the work we did over the years.

Shortly after college, she got a job in New York City, and she met Marcus. He was different. He was the real deal. Finally she found someone where there seemed like a future beyond what was convenient; someone who could get serious.

After dating several months and with everything going great, Marcus showed up at her place unannounced one evening. He said he needed to talk. He explained how he felt like things were "moving too quickly" and he wanted "to slow things down and be more casual." Hannah was devastated. It was happening again. In the past, she would have swallowed her tears and acted fine with it, saying, "It's okay," and then have a long talk to make him feel better to at least preserve the hope that it might work out.

This time was different though. Those days were gone. Instead of cowering to fear, she cut him off about forty-five seconds into his rambling explanation and excuses and said loud and clearly, "Sounds like you don't know what you want. But I do. I deserve to be with someone who wants to be with me, no questions asked. So since that's not what you want, you can leave now." He started to try and reply, but she just pointed at the door and said two words: "Get out!"

Marcus was shocked and tried again to make peace, but Hannah would have nothing of it. "There's nothing more to talk about. Get out!" she repeated, until with a stunned look on his face, he finally left a minute later.

She immediately called me and broke down in tears. I was standing in a parking garage in San Francisco when I took the call. I can still remember the looks on the faces of a few people walking by as I started jumping up and down cheering her on, even through her tears. "Hannah! You did it! You found your voice! You sent a message to the whole damn world today that you are done wasting time! You literally just changed your life ..."

Before we got off the call, I cautioned her to be prepared. There was an eight in ten chance that Marcus would be texting her and wanting to talk and most likely within twenty-four hours. I told her that under no condition was she to agree to meet him to talk further until at least two weeks had gone by, and even then, it could only be over lunch at a public place. She needed to ensure that his begging for another chance was coming from clarity in him and not fear. She needed to ensure whatever decision she would make then, needed to be from clarity too.

He was back in contact within twenty-four hours. They met for lunch but only five days later.

That was three and half years ago.

They are getting married next October.

She was ready. He was the one who needed to cross the bridge beyond the next and final stage of adolescence ... the step of going 100% all in!

Let's go there now too.

chapter
nine

Crossing the Third Bridge:
Commitment and Career
"Am I Ready? Am I Good Enough?"

George hated his job. He hated serving steaks to high-maintenance customers at Outback Steakhouse, working for an unreliable manager, dealing with coworkers who lacked work ethic, and barely making enough money to keep up with expenses. He was twenty-three. He'd dropped out of college after drinking his way through freshman year. He'd attended a very competitive high school, stressed his way through classes that were both too hard and too uninteresting to him, and, by the time he started college, was just burned out on school.

Few people realize how common George's college experience is. Colleges and universities certainly do not advertise it. Nationally, 30 percent of incoming college freshman drop out after their first year. Over 56 percent do not have a degree six years later. More than 50 percent of grads move back home after college because they are unable to earn enough to live on their own and are unsure of what they want to do or are not really equipped to function as autonomous adults.

This entire demographic of young adults in their early twenties is the fastest growing segment of my client base. They are among the most interesting and exciting to work with; worldly enough and bright enough to learn at a fast pace, and are often highly motivated. Not many people this age want to be sitting at home, getting spending money from their parents, having to tell a date not to come over because their parents are awake. In this day and age that's pretty discouraging if not humiliating.

Young adults in this stage are in one of four places:

- They feel lost, having no idea what they want to do with their lives.

- They have ideas but are not sure which direction to go.

- They know what they want but are feeling overwhelmed by the task ahead.

- They know what they want, have a plan, and feel ready to implement it.

The functional questions they need answers to always include:

- What do I want to be doing?

- Where do I want to be doing it?

- Who do I want to associate with?

- What is the path to getting there?

The deeper driving question—the one that guards the last big threshold into adulthood, comes after all the others are answered. It is: "Am I ready for this?" or sometimes "Am I good enough?"

Frequently, when I meet older teens or young adults in this stage, they claim to not know what they want to be doing. This group is often still stuck in Stage 2 of the journey to adulthood. Almost as frequently, though, I meet the ones who know what they want but are feeling overwhelmed at the volume of work and/or risk it will take to do it.

That describes where George was when I met him. Just before I met him, a roommate had failed to pay rent. Suddenly, after three years of living on his own, he was forced to move back into his childhood bedroom with his parents. His mom insisted George meet me as a condition of their letting him stay with them. Getting "help" was certainly not his idea. When she and I spoke on the phone I could hear the mix between concern for son and frustration with him. These mixed feelings are common in parents who have young adult children who are steeped in the "failure to launch" pattern.

George agreed to meet me, sending me an email asking to schedule an appointment. When he showed up, he made it clear right away that he would approach this with an open mind but that he wasn't the kind of guy who was into talking about his problems, that he was only here because his parents insisted that he meet me and for now, he needed their financial support so he really had no choice.

Instead of talking about his "problems," I focused the conversation on his interests. It took me all of about twenty minutes to figure out that this guy wasn't a food server; he was a car guy. Let me be clear; there are numerous kinds of car guys, everything from novice thrill seekers to collectors to performance drivers and many things in between. "Men and their machines" is a well-worn cliché. But George was not a thrill seeker, and while he would probably love to drive a Lamborghini around the Indianapolis Speedway, most of us would too. George was what I eventually dubbed a Blue Collar Artist™.

He loved customizing cars. He would spend an entire night and day patiently trying to fit a new piece of molding into his car. His curiosity to figure out how to do it was as intense as his desire to do it right. Any modification he could do to his car on his own, he would do. Anything that had to be done by a shop, he would hover in the background watching them do it, learning and satisfying his curiosity.

This wasn't a guy who should be stuck saving his money to have some one else put new rims on his Lexus. This was a guy who should be building toward mastery to become the most skilled Blue Collar Artist doing this work.

The conversation in this first meeting quickly got very serious. "Why are you waiting tables instead of training to be a specialist in working on cars?"

"How am I supposed to do that? What are you suggesting, I should go get a job changing oil somewhere?"

"No. I am suggesting that you seriously consider getting formal training to do what you already are doing, and then find a way to get paid to do it professionally."

It was August 10th. The next semester of courses in the automobile tech program at the local community college began in fourteen days. He enrolled.

A few months later he got a job customizing cars. He was an apprentice, getting paid peanuts, but at the same time he was in the rare club of people who actually get paid to do what they love. Slowly he built confidence in himself that he could do this work. For the first time in his life he started getting straight As in school.

Now our conversations went from getting jobs in this industry to creating jobs in this industry.

This waiter at Outback Steakhouse was going from serving blooming onions to filing for business licenses, writing a business plan, finding investors, seeking out commercial property, designing marketing materials, investing in his training, managing customer expectations, and getting an MBA course the old-fashioned way, by doing it in the real world.

Probably fifty times during that two-year journey from waiter to business owner, we had conversations that addressed the "Am I good enough?" question, from "Can I pass this math class when I barely passed math in high school?" to "Can I actually do this customization on this car this customer brought in?" … "Can I have this difficult conversation with my investor?" Again and again, we walked through the process that led to his finally having the trust in himself and his abilities. Though the details are unique to each individual, the questions are always the same.

Sophie's Voice

Did this prominent PR firm understand that this rising young star they were promoting barely graduated college? Did they know about the math course she had to take four times at the University of Arizona before she passed it? Did they know about the string of "bad boys" she dated before she finally decided they weren't for her? Did they know the number of times her father had threatened to cut her off financially or how often friends sat her down to talk about their concerns about her, all just a few short years ago?

Did they know that her whole writing career began with a naughty little blog she wrote about the life of a sexy, sassy blond sorority girl and the exploits and sexploits of her and her friends? Did they know that she started it mostly for attention? How else do you come up with a name for a blog like *Party Like You're Famous?*

Little did she know that this little blog (don't bother searching for it, as it has long since been taken down) would catch fire in the world of Millennials, going from a few friends who read it daily to an audience of thousands worldwide, which led to offers from firms that needed people who could write to Millennials, to internships, and ultimately to job offers writing for PR firms that focus on helping companies market to her generation.

Now here she was, twenty-three years old, less than a year out of college after a mediocre academic experience, being called into the boss's office to find out she has been promoted to an account manager and would be overseeing two employees on her team (both older and more experienced than she), working with one of their biggest and most important accounts. It's no wonder she smiled nervously and said all the right things in the meeting with her boss and then immediately ran to the bathroom to text the people close to her, telling them how anxious she was.

I was one of the people who got a text: *"Can you talk ASAP? Need to talk NOW!"*

"How am I supposed to do this?" she questioned. "I've never supervised anyone! I am only twenty-three years old. I haven't even been out of college one year." The fact that her performance reviews had been stellar and that she was the darling new hire of her nationally acclaimed boss, mattered little. Sophie's self-doubt had a long history that was both personal and universal. While she was several years removed now from the dark days of partying like she's famous and barely passing her courses, the sting of the memory of how much she'd doubted herself back then, and what she had been through personally returned at times like this. She'd gone to an academically competitive public high school and sat in classes for years with kids who went on to many of the nation's elite colleges and universities. Two of her close friends went to Ivy League schools. She'd always felt not as smart, not as capable, and not as worthy.

That's a hard thing to break free from, and the personal burden she carries. But there is another one, a much bigger one and a much more universal one that shows up at this stage. Like George, Sophie was also grappling with the final threshold to adulthood question of her own worthiness, capability, and readiness.

My conversation with her that day was a brief one. I reminded her in no uncertain terms that her crazy high school and college years helped her find a writer's voice that has mass appeal to her generation, that businesses who are hungry to market to this age group struggled to find someone who could speak to them in a way that appealed to them, that she was a hot commodity, and that anyone who wanted to know how to communicate with Millennials has a lot to learn from her, including the two coworkers she would be supervising.

I reminded her that the willingness to ask questions and draw on her resources, like she was doing in making this call to me, was what was going to ensure she learned how to handle management issues effectively, and her willingness to boldly stay on her path in life is what would ensure she'd do just fine.

Lastly I pointed out that very few people are naturally good at managing others. I explained to her that after sales training, management training was the biggest training investment most companies make. They had to make this investment because it didn't come naturally to most people.

She was much calmer after our twenty minutes on the phone.

No surprise, she succeeded in her new position.

The next call I got from her was months later, after she saw a whole bunch of former classmates from high school and realized that she was one of the most advanced in her career and one of the few who actually liked what she was doing: "It was pretty crazy to find out how many of these guys who went to colleges I could never have gotten into were back home couch surfing, working retail, or just working in their dad's business, living for the weekends and still partying like they were in college. I felt like I could hardly relate to most of them. I feel so lucky."

It wasn't long before headhunters started calling and offering her interviews in much higher paying jobs in bigger, more prestigious firms. Now, while she still has the pings of doubt and "Am I ready for this?" questions, they are less intense, shorter lived and less relevant.

"A little of questioning your readiness and ability," I suggested to her, "is good. It keeps you humble and focused on learning. It will keep you from taking the wrong job, and it will keep you on your toes. But never get lost in making more meaning out of it than is useful. So far, in the domain you are moving in professionally, you are more than ready, more than good enough, and more than capable. Don't take my word for it. Trust the evidence."

From $120K to Starting Over

Twenty-four-year-old Nathan graduated with a degree in computer science from a prominent university. He immediately accepted a $120,000-a-year job working for a well-known tech company.

After just six weeks, he quit.

He hated the corporate culture. They were vultures, without ethics. Every meeting was about how can we exploit this and monetize that. The people he worked with were only fixated on money, getting their share and getting ahead.

"It's not like I expected everyone to want to save the world," he explained, "but when data comes in that shows how to hook nine-year-olds on games and no one is asking if the game is good for them, I just couldn't be part of it."

Many Millennials share Nathan's moral conviction. They want to ensure that what they do contributes in some kind of positive way.

Seven months had gone by since he quit the job. He's been living in his parent's home, oscillating between playing video games, working out at the gym, socializing with a few peers, and on occasion pursuing some networking opportunities that had come his way. He was struggling to keep his spirits up.

He was another poster child for the "failure to launch" subset of his generation, one of the growing number of college graduates who are back home, unsure what they want to do with their lives or unable or unwilling to do what it would takes to get launched. I designed my HeroPath® Launch (www.HeroPathLaunch.com) program just for them.

There are many factors that contribute to why these young adults are in these circumstances. Many of them are like Nathan—bright, well-educated, capable—and struggling. Many of them just feel lost. Many wind up spending their days playing video games, smoking weed, feeling disconnected, and losing momentum. Others are aggressively trying to get interviews, feeling like they are on a roller coaster of hope and possibilities, followed by disappointments.

I've met many of them in the past few years. My heart goes out to the ones who are trying hard but not finding it easy. It is not their fault they came out of college in such difficult times. Sometimes I share their anger at the education system that put them through immense stress to qualify to attend colleges that granted their degrees but didn't prepare them for the real world. Sometimes their anger is warranted; other times it is just a convenient excuse. Everyone must learn how to function in the world as it is. Pointing fingers and laying blame is rarely a good use of time and energy. Learning how to make things work and to get results in spite of obstacles, always is.

For someone like Nathan who had connections but had gotten disconnected and disconcerted by his one bad experience in the corporate world, the first order of business was to re-engage him in the quest to move beyond the threshold of the stage of life he was in, so he could cross the bridge to the next one. Nathan wasn't at the "Am I good enough?" phase yet. He was stuck in the "Who am I, what do I want, and where do I fit in in the world?" phase. So that is where we started.

The nice thing about working with people his age is that they typically have more than enough reference life experiences to help them quickly find answers to their questions. This enables them to narrow the range of their options quickly. As I describe in the previous section of the book, this is much harder to do with someone like Anna, the girl who always came in second place. At just sixteen years old, she needed to have more life experiences in order to understand herself. Nathan had more than enough life experiences; he just didn't realize how valuable they actually were.

There is a frame of reference for thinking about how life works and a line of questioning I follow with participants in my HeroPath® programs. It very quickly helps older teens and young adults identify enough valuable self-knowledge to start making healthy life direction decisions for themselves. This is what I did with Nathan. After just a few conversations, it was clear that his interest was in the technology field, particularly around the video game industry. It was clear he was interested in business. It was clear he had a deep sense of ethics and morality, of right and wrong, and valued this to the degree that it was actually impeding him, though for what I would argue are good reasons.

It was also clear that he was stuck inside his own head and was not keeping his actions and attention out in the world where it needed to be.

One of the last, yet most challenging and significant thresholds to cross from childhood to adulthood is the threshold of commitment to something bigger than oneself. It comes easier for some than for others, but it always comes at a cost. Making this kind of commitment means giving up excuses, options, and comforts that keep a person stuck in a stage of life. If it is commitment in relationship, it means giving up the chance to be with everyone else. If it is commitment to a career, it means giving up everything else to pursue mastery in this one thing. The critical commitment that Nathan needed to make was the commitment to making a contribution to the world, rather than continuing to just live off his parents. It was the commitment to begin offering value to someone else, in exchange for them sharing value in return.

As I explained this to him, I could see he got it. He knew it was time to stop making decisions that were solely about him and to start making decisions that were about what he could bring to the world. That is an enormous threshold to cross. Within weeks of making this commitment, three potential job options were available to him. Two of them were straightforward, well-paying jobs in the tech field. The third was a wild card that involved helping someone build a start-up that would do work right at the intersection of all the things that interested hm. While the viability of the company hinged on many unknowns, the certainty that it was intriguing was absolute. But lacking any real business leadership background, he doubted himself. Nonetheless, the founder of the company liked him and valued what he brought to the table. He was tech savvy and knew the gaming side as a consumer and a strategist.

"I think I'll go with the first job," he told me. Then he proceeded to tell me why, each of the reasons amounting to variations of how much more predictable and certain he was that he could succeed.

"Let me ask you an unusual question," I began. "When you think about the start-up and consider it as an option, do you say no to it because it just doesn't feel right to you or because of something else? Other than the certainty of long-term funding, it seems to be the most intriguing opportunity."

"It is," he agreed, "but I just don't know if I could succeed at it. I don't know that I am ready to step into such a significant position without years of experience."

"Interesting. In my experience the internal response that says 'yes' but is accompanied by 'Am I ready for this?' or 'Am I good enough?' is often the response that means you are on the right path. It is the benchmark questioning that a person goes through as they are making the last big step into adulthood."

He took that in, quiet for a long moment. When he finally spoke, he said, "I think you are totally right. Deep down I know this is the right option to choose. I know that other than some pride and some time, I have nothing to lose. It's such a big step to go from sitting on my parents' couch to being a founder of a potentially very big company. It feels so ... grown-up!"

"Welcome to the big leagues," I replied. "You *are* a grown-up."

He stood taller after that. He held his own in meetings and negotiations and accepted the challenge that comes with being on a steep learning curve. Whether or not the company makes it remains uncertain. What is certain is that he knows he made the right choice to face his fear and move forward with it.

A few months later I told him, "Crossing the 'Am I ready for this?' career threshold to adulthood is only one part of it. Remember, there is also the relationship and commitment 'Am I ready for this?' threshold, too!"

"One step at a time, man. One step at a time!" he answered.

So long as the steps are on the right path for the individual, I couldn't agree more.

A Woman's Flaws Disappeared Overnight

27 year old Blake, was highly educated, having graduated from a top tier university with honors. He was successful in his career and was in the beginning stages of launching his own consulting practice in New York City. Professionally, he was confident and competent and knew he was good enough and ready. His "problem" was that the woman he was dating, wanted to get married! He not only didn't feel ready, he wasn't sure she was the right person. She was as educated, worldly, and successful in her own career as he was in his. Sure, she had her quirks, but so did he, and so does everyone.

One of the pieces of advice I most often share with young adults regarding marriage is to let go of the Hugh Grant/Hollywood romantic comedy notion that their life partner has to be their all and everything. We are all complex, with many interests and needs, and have different people in our lives to fill those needs. I explain how I have certain friends I talk to and do things with that my wife has no interest in, and she has her own friends with whom she shares interests that I have no interest in. What matters is that we do share the core things needed to build a life and raise a healthy family. But the bigger challenge that a guy like Blake faced was letting go of all options to just embrace one.

It took him a long time to integrate the message from the conversations we had that year. He grappled with it, pondered it, spoke to many others about it, and eventually surrendered to it. He loved her. He knew she was the one. So he made the commitment, and the moment he did, even before he proposed to her, everything began to change. She was suddenly much more relaxed. She was suddenly much less negative. The list went on.

A few months into their engagement, he sent me this email:

> Hey Jeff -
>
> Wanted to shoot you a quick note and say thank you.
>
> A while back, when talking about my girlfriend, you mentioned how totally diving in would change things. You probably sensed this at the time, but I totally thought you were full of it, haha. I was like, "that Jeff, he's so strangely conservative sometimes."
>
> But, you know what? That advice was totally spot on. Things have been wonderful since taking the next step, totally wonderful, better than I ever could have imagined...

As I explained to him, one of the fundamental things about being human is that our primary instinct is to survive. Our next instinct is to keep the species alive, and our third-level instinct is to evolve and thrive.

Whenever a person feels unsafe, they default to survival mode. In the extreme, this means "fight or flight"—often quite literally. More sophisticated people do "fight or flight" differently. They play games, make excuses, rationalize, justify, and just behave badly. If she was behaving this way, very likely it was because she did not feel safe with him or feel that she could fully trust him.

The moment she could, everything changed.

How we are with others impacts how they are with us. We are an interdependent species. If we take this concept into the bigger world beyond Blake's hesitation impacting his girlfriend, we see this dynamic play out everywhere we turn. Because the focus of my professional life the past twenty-five years has been on the development of youth as they move through adolescence into adulthood, I see this phenomenon everywhere I turn. So often, adolescents negative behaviors are a directly result of the degree to which they feel like they are in a fight for their survival. Whether these negative behaviors show up as aggression, drug use, lack of motivation, depression, worry, or other stress reactions, they are almost always associated with the degree to which the teen feels like they are fighting for their survival.

When I worked with youth from impoverished backgrounds and neighborhoods filled with real violence, I understood why they were so guarded, so defensive, so aggressive, or so hard to reach. Their literal survival depended on protecting themselves.

Most of the teens and young adults I have written about here have a different perception of survival, albeit one that feels just as intense and real. They are fighting to survive socially, academically, and eventually, monetarily. Too often they feel like everything is a competition for scarce resources and scarce opportunities. The distorted message about how few pathways there are to finding professional success, only further reinforces survival and self-absorption.

Because of this, teaching them to keep their perspective, their sense of humor, and their sense of possibilities intact becomes critical to their success in life and our success in helping them. What that translates to is that even in their deepest and darkest struggles, they must learn to stay open, creative, and forward thinking and to never give up. In this age of dystopian themes running through popular entertainment, blogs, and news, orienting this way runs counterculture.

Because I do not believe that every child *needs* to go to an elite college (or even go to college at all, necessarily), needs to have a booming social life, needs to find a passion, or needs to find a valid reason why they are learning certain things in school, my work is not for everyone. I also firmly believe that if more adults who are helping to raise youth would open their minds up and focus instead on helping youth build on their strengths and interests, instead of on trying so hard to shape them into people who will fit into the narrow categories of conventional success, they would have much greater credibility and effectiveness in helping youth to thrive.

Too Many Choices

There is a common intention many parents and educators hold to help youth "keep all their options open". I find this to be a very bad strategy. Instead we should encourage them to eliminate options that are not and will never be the right ones for them. Often this is discouraged because of the likelihood of being able to make it financially in many careers they may find most appealing, so they are encouraged to have the proverbial "back-up plan".

Beyond Back-Up Plans

Randy was a prodigious child actor. He went to UCLA's acting school and graduated in three years. When he graduated, one of his professors offered this wise advice: "Do what you need to do to pay the bills. It is okay to wait tables. But just make sure you put in an equal amount of hours practicing your acting, as you do working in some other job."

He followed his professor's advice and he had to live in the real world of trying to be an actor in LA. "I would see these calls for audition seeking someone who was '5'10", blond hair, blue eyes, baritone voice' and get all excited. They described me perfectly. Then I would show up for the audition and sit in a room with a hundred other guys who were 5'10" blond haired blue eyed with baritone voices! It was disheartening at times, but I followed my Professor's advice and just kept practicing hard and showing up!" Eventually he got parts in a few smaller stage productions, and joined the tiny fraction of people on earth who ever got paid to do something they truly loved.

A year later he applied to graduate school at Arizona State's Walter Cronkite School of Journalism and Mass Communication He was a natural behind the mic and in front of the camera. He began by calling sports games, then was invited to host a daily sports news broadcast. A year later he was offered a job as a sports and news broadcaster for an ABC affiliate in Oregon. He thrived there and recently moved on to a much larger market in Alabama. He finds the work intellectually and creatively stimulating. He works with a tight knit team of people who believe in what they do and care about the service they provide for their viewers. He's a bit of a local celebrity, but more than anything he is a model of what happens when a person follows their interests and their strengths, and finds out where they can lead. Southern Oregon and Tuscaloosa, Alabama is not the glamour and glitz of Hollywood, but they have proven to be a wonderful place to work and raise his young family… and that, he has long since discovered, is far more important to him than anything else.

Where will the life journeys of all the teens and young adults I've written about in this book lead them? That remains to be seen. The evidence is though that by approaching their life with openness, building on their strengths and interests, becoming more savvy, honoring the things about themselves that are constant and will not change, doing the work to change and improve upon the ones that can change and be improved, and making excellent choices, their lives will be rich adventures, and their contributions will match or exceed what they take – the way it always is for the people who stay true to their path, act with courage and uncompromising conviction to their values and continue to learn and update to the times and world they live in.

I truly believe in the old African proverb that "It takes a village." For me personally, the role I play in the lives of my clients is both highly professional and deeply personal. Over the years I have gone to my clients' concerts, games, graduation ceremonies, Bar Mitzvahs, birthdays and sadly, the funerals of some of their parents. Fortunately I've also been to far more of their weddings too (once even officiating one).

It was at one of these weddings that a realization came to me. I was standing in front of the gathering of friends and family, speaking to Todd and Karen, with their parents standing right behind them.

I looked at their parents and something occurred to me. "You know when our children are born they are totally dependent, totally helpless, and yet totally filled with potential. As parents we do the best we can, and we often do not know if what we are doing is right or if it will be good enough. Well, the fact that Todd and Karen have found each other and are standing here today means you have done your job. They are ready to be on their own, to make their own home and a family of their own. From this day on, *though they will always be your son and daughter, they are no longer your children.*"

Isn't that what we all want and what we all should be aspiring to do—to raise our children to no longer be children? To do so, we must restore health and sanity to the journey through the adolescent years.

We must take it back from a system that too often treats it like a disease or tries to fit every child into the same formula. We must give our children the resources and experiences they need to progress through the stages and emerge as adults, like Blake, Sophie, Mateo, Randy and George are, and that Christopher, Leah, Faheem, Anna, Nick, Kenneth, Gabrielle, Kelsey, Nathan, Hayden, Nico, Tanner, Lindsey, Jared, Michelle, and Jenny are well on their way to becoming.

I can't think of anything more important to be doing.

chapter
ten

One Last Story to Open a Door: Riley's Visit to the Post Office

Occasionally a client comes along who has a love/hate relationship with me and my work, and the feeling becomes mutual. Most professionals who work with youth can relate. These clients are such a hassle to work with that I have to fight myself to put up with their evasiveness. And I am often equally as annoying to them, because no matter how hard they try, they can't prove I offer no value.

Typically they are the ones who are the least likely to seek out someone to talk to. Usually this is because of pride, stubbornness, or some agenda against their parents. They come in dragging their heals, determined to ensure the work I do fails, determined to prove I am just like everyone else and that they do not need the help.

Then we start to work together, and it isn't that bad. Over time, I prove I know what I'm talking about. Given the option to call it quits, something inside them tells them to stay the course. They know deep down that that this is good for them and it is what they need; it's just not easy to own up to that and do the work.

Riley and I met when he was in eighth grade. He participated in a mentoring group I did for a small group of boys at his middle school. We met again two years later when he was caught getting drunk at a public park. His parents had grounded him, and one of the conditions for getting ungrounded was that he had to "meet with" someone. He had a fiery temper, intense mood swings, and an artist's temperament. He was also tall, good-looking, athletic, outgoing, "one of the guys," and at the same time sensitive, creative, and an old soul.

Trusting her instinct, his mom reached out to me. She remembered me from the group I'd run a few years earlier and just had a sense that Riley needed a mentor, not a psychologist. I could write a book about the journey in the work with him because it truly was a journey for both of us.

After working with him for about six months in which he canceled or rescheduled appointments with me about a dozen times, enough was enough. I called his parents and told them I either needed to stop working with him or do something radical. They chose radical.

Three weeks later he was on an airplane with me flying to London. I was running a HeroPath® program with a group of teens from England, Ireland, Spain, and Denmark. He went because it was a trip to London and a chance to meet some of his peers from overseas.

When we returned, I sent him an email titled "24 Hour Notice." In it, I told him that he had to make a final decision. Either he was "all-in" with me, or he was out and we would not speak again, ever. He had to let me know by 5 p.m. the next day. Being "all-in" meant answering my text messages, keeping appointments, reaching out to me, and following through on things we talked about. It meant being open and honest with me and letting me into his life without making me work so damn hard.

He freaked out. He called his dad at work. He called his mom three times that day from school. He finally sent me a text asking if we could talk about this in person. I picked him up after school, and we drove up to a spectacular cliff overlooking the Pacific Ocean. He paced back and forth and grappled with the situation he was in. To be all-in meant commitment. It meant growing up.

"Jeff, can we meet up here all the time from now on?" he asked me, looking out over the ocean. It was his way of saying, "I'm in." He was just turning seventeen years old. He was on the threshold of manhood but not yet there.

That following Thanksgiving, he met Sara. She was the cousin of one his friends and was visiting from Oregon. Riley hit it off with Sara like he never had before with a girl. She was cool beyond words. She loved surfing. She loved the same music. They had chemistry. The last night she was in town, they stayed up talking until 5 o'clock in the morning. Then he needed to go home before his parents woke up and realized he hadn't come home that night. She walked him to the door. Should he kiss her, should he hug her, should he say something? He was so nervous he couldn't figure out what to do. So in an awkward moment, she kissed him on the cheek, and he hugged her, and he walked away feeling stupid.

When I woke up that morning, there was a series of text messages from him: *"Jeff, we need to meet, like right now!"*

When we met later that day, he told me the story, concerned that he'd blown his chance because not kissing her sent a message that he wasn't into her. He was concerned he was being stupid because she lived so far away and they were too young to make it work, whatever "it" was.

I asked him the one question every one of my clients comes to love and hate, "What do you want?"

"Jeff, man, c'mon," he replied anxiously. "I want you to tell me what I want!" Knowing that answer wouldn't fly, he finally just said it: "I like her. I want her to know that."

"I can tell you what I would do," I replied. "But I know you won't do it."

"Don't do that reverse psychology shit on me, man!" he yelled.

"Riley, I am not doing any reverse psychology shit!" I yelled back. "I am telling you that you won't do it and I don't blame you, because it will probably backfire and you will walk away looking like a fool!"

"What is it?" he asked, demanding an answer.

"You both like music, so I'd do something like this: I would burn a CD with your favorite music, write her a letter telling her how you feel, stick them in an envelope, and mail it to her."

"Burn a CD? Write a letter? Are you fucking crazy?" he shouted back at me. "Do you know how much crap I will get from everyone if I do that and she tells her cousin, who I know will tell everyone! And no one burns CDs anymore!"

Riley, like many clients I work with, has no hesitation in saying what's on his mind exactly the way he wants to say it.

"I told you you wouldn't do it," I replied. "And I told you it would probably backfire."

"Then why are you even suggesting it?" he asked.

"Because it's what I think you should do. If you want to send a girl a message that she is special to you, then you have to do something over and above."

"You are fucking nuts, man," he mumbled, repeating under his breath, "no one sends CDs and love letters anymore!" Then he got quiet, and drifted off into thought. He stayed quiet for a good minute and a half. Suddenly he sat up, leaned forward, pounded his hand into his fist and yelled out, *"Fuck It Jeff!!! Every guy wants to write this letter! I'm going to do it!"*

And he did. He went to the post office and mailed it. He texted me about a dozen times from the post office. In this age of email and texting, it was actually his first time ever being there. A first time for everything.

Often, when I tell people this story, they want to know what happened. Did she write back? Did they get together? Are they married? Did she tell her cousin? Did he make a fool of himself? What happened after isn't the point. The point is that *he did it*. He stepped up, faced his fear, and acted like the man he really wanted to be … and he did it regardless of what anyone else might think or say if they found out. He did what it took to find out if there was really something there with Sara.

That day, he left his boyhood behind. He crossed the bridge to the next stage of his life.

That was seven years ago. I had dinner with Riley a few weeks ago in Austin, Texas. He is twenty-four now, having graduated with a degree in advertising from the University of Texas and taken a job working for an up-and-coming advertising firm. I told him I would be using this story in this book, and he told me to not only use it but to use his real name. Riley is damn proud of the work he did to stop being an impulsive, moody adolescent ... and with his work ethic, creative talent, and charisma, no doubt the best is yet to come.

I have met so many Rileys over time, many of them teen and young adult boys and girls who no one ever thought would "talk" to someone yet when the right help came along, they not only talked, they listened.

If something in what you've read here resonates with you and you would like to learn more about how we might work together, please contact my office. The direct contact information is listed on the next page. Evolution Mentoring® is a very exclusive private customized mentoring relationship that is especially potent for the teen or young adult who is bright, thoughtful and seeking more depth and substance in life. HeroPath® is a workshop and coaching program for older teens and young adults who are seeking answers to the critical Life Direction questions. Everything I do and the team of coaches I have trained will do, is positively biased, educational in nature and flows from this one underlying belief: Growing into adulthood shouldn't be something to stress and worry about, it should be an adventure to lived, where the best is yet to come.

It takes a Village. It would be an honor to join yours and to include you in ours. Contact us to learn more.

Next Steps

Evolution Mentoring* Private Mentoring with Jeffrey Leiken

Contact Jeffrey Leiken

www.EvolutionMentoring.com

HeroPath® Training And Coaching

For Older Teens & Young Adults –

Find Life Direction & Tools For Success

Learn more:

www.HeroPath.life

Jeffrey is available for conferences, keynotes, parent education, and professional development.

He can be directly reached at:

Jeff@Leiken.com

415.441.8218

Printed in the USA
CPSIA information can be obtained
at www.ICGtesting.com
JSHW012052140824
68134JS00035B/3386

9 781599 326344